Inside | Out

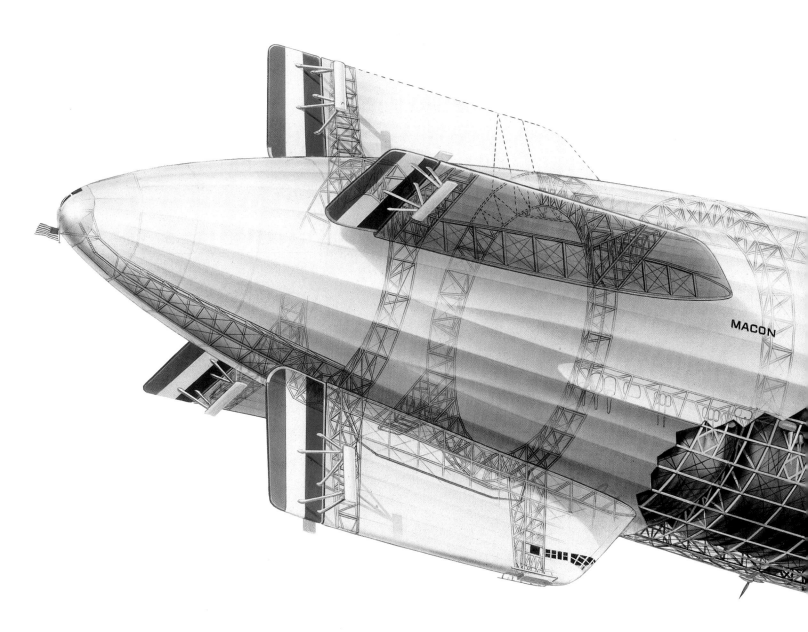

Inside|Out

The Best of National Geographic
Diagrams and Cutaways

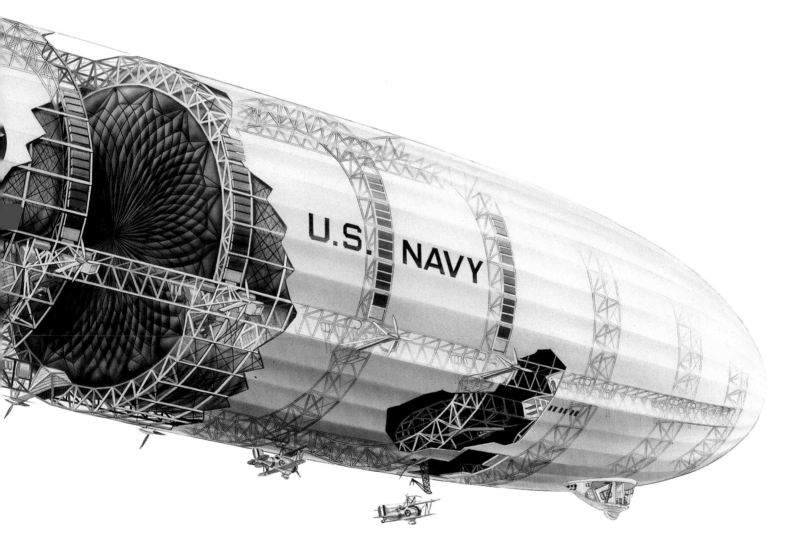

NATIONAL
GEOGRAPHIC
SOCIETY

WASHINGTON, D. C.

INSIDE | OUT
The Best of National Geographic Diagrams and Cutaways

Published by The National Geographic Society

John M. Fahey, Jr.	*President and Chief Executive Officer*
Gilbert M. Grosvenor	*Chairman of the Board*
Nina D. Hoffman	*Senior Vice President*

Prepared by The Book Division

William R. Gray	*Vice President and Director*
Charles Kogod	*Assistant Director*
Barbara A. Payne	*Editorial Director and Managing Editor*
David Griffin	*Design Director*

Staff for this book

Project Editor	David Griffin
Text Editor	Rebecca Lescaze
Art Director	Suez Kehl Corrado
Researcher	Elizabeth Cook Thompson
Contributing Writers	Christopher P. Sloan, Karen E. Gibbs
Project Consultant	Allen Carroll
Production Project Manager	Lewis R. Bassford
Staff Assistants	Barbara Bricks, Peggy Candore, Kris Hannah, Holly Legler, Beverly Taylor

Manufacturing and Quality Control

George V. White	*Director*
John T. Dunn	*Associate Director*
Polly P. Tompkins	*Executive Assistant*

Library of Congress CIP Data

Inside/out : the best of National Geographic diagrams and cutaways /
  [prepared by the Book Division of National Geographic Society].
    p.   cm.
  ISBN 0-7922-7371-0
  1. National geographic--Publishing.   2. Magazine design.
  3. Design (Printing)   I. National Geographic Society (U.S.).   Book Division.
  G3.N37157 1998
  686.2'252--dc21   98-4636

Preceding pages: Illustration of the U.S.S. *Macon* by Richard and Kent Leech.
NATIONAL GEOGRAPHIC—January 1992

CONTENTS

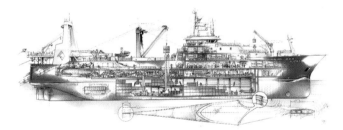

The Diagram
at National Geographic

By Christopher P. Sloan

Art Director, NATIONAL GEOGRAPHIC

THE DIAGRAM ARTWORK of the National Geographic Society serves as a lens and a mirror. Through the lens we peer at hidden worlds and see things that would otherwise be impossible to see. In the mirror we see reflected the state of scientific knowledge, whether of 20 years ago or of today. A diagram starts with the need to explain something. Greek mathematicians, needing to explain geometry, coined the word *diagramma*—to mark with lines—for their drawings. Today, we use the word loosely to refer to an enormous array of explanatory images from astronomical to zoological.

According to Edward Tufte, an authority on information design, the special power of diagrams lies in their "capacity to show places or activities that we are unable to see directly from one fixed viewpoint in the real world." Photographers at the National Geographic Society are among the most talented in the world, but they are limited by the "fixed viewpoint" of their cameras. This is where diagrams come in. If a photographer can't get it on film, or if a writer can't describe it efficiently in words, it's time for art to re-create it.

At the Society, a staff of art directors and researchers and a cadre of freelance illustrators make a special effort to take our readers to places photography can't go. Our diagrams complement the words and photographs so as to convey the whole picture. We peer into the past. We zoom into the human body. We probe outer space. Sometimes, like NATIONAL GEOGRAPHIC photographers and writers, we stay on earth and travel to places like Africa or China—or Homestead, Florida—to do our work.

In the summer of 1992 I found myself standing in Pinewood Village near Homestead, Florida, days after Hurricane Andrew ripped through Dade County. I was there as art director for a major article the magazine was planning on the disaster. Pinewood Village was one of the places where hurricane winds cranked up to more than 300 miles per hour, generating mini-vortices that mowed through homes like buzz saws. Now the homes stood sad and deserted with gaping wounds in them. Sofas, lamps, rugs, and toys lay scattered in tortured positions on the grass.

With the chaos of the hurricane in front of me it was hard to imagine any diagram that could explain the cause. In the immediate aftermath of the disaster, scientists at the National Hurricane Center in Miami and other research centers were busy studying measurements, maps, and models of the hurricane to make sense of what had happened. The best way to get information was for me to visit them at their workplace for a firsthand look. On assignment, an art director has to be like a sponge, soaking up as much information as possible from experts and from personal observation. Diagrams, photographs, maps from scientists, and books are all grist for the mill and will be used later as an illustration develops.

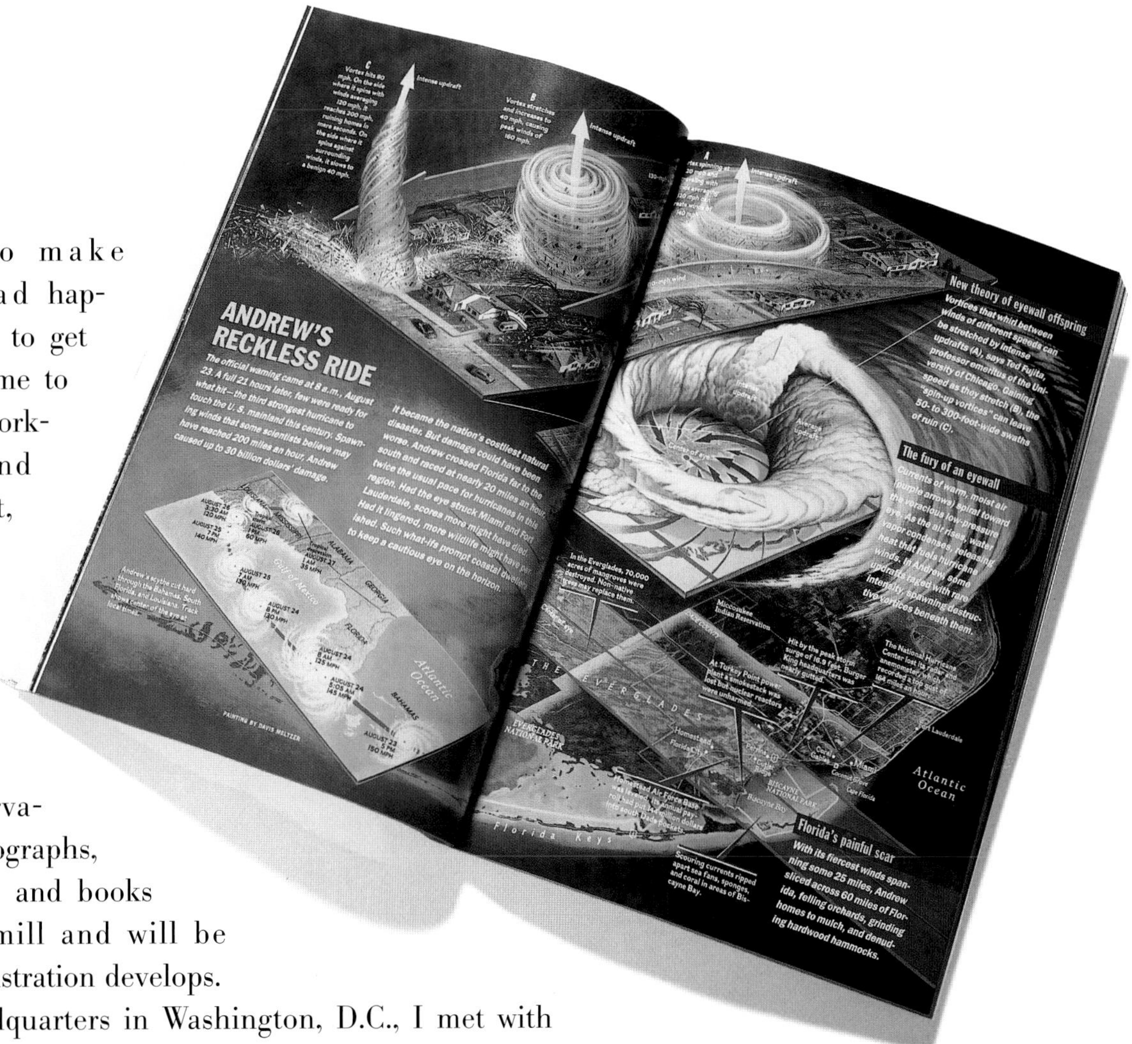

Figure 1: Davis Meltzer illustrated the aftermath of Hurricane Andrew for an article in the April 1993 NATIONAL GEOGRAPHIC magazine.

Back at our headquarters in Washington, D.C., I met with veteran artist Davis Meltzer and art researcher Karen Gibbs. Every diagram in NATIONAL GEOGRAPHIC has such a team. I shared with them all of the material I had brought back and discussed my thoughts about what kind of diagram we needed to develop. Meltzer's job was to work with me to develop a dramatic, informative diagram (Figure 1 and pages 80-81). Gibbs's responsibility was to obtain new information and work closely with experts to make certain every detail of the diagram was correct.

A NATIONAL GEOGRAPHIC diagram and its accompanying words are designed closely together, sometimes integrating cartography as well. Labels, notes, and captions are carefully written and placed on the artwork, using a computerized publishing system.

The Drive for Accuracy

NATIONAL GEOGRAPHIC artwork exemplifies the Society's long-standing commitment to quality and accuracy. It is one of few organizations willing to go to great

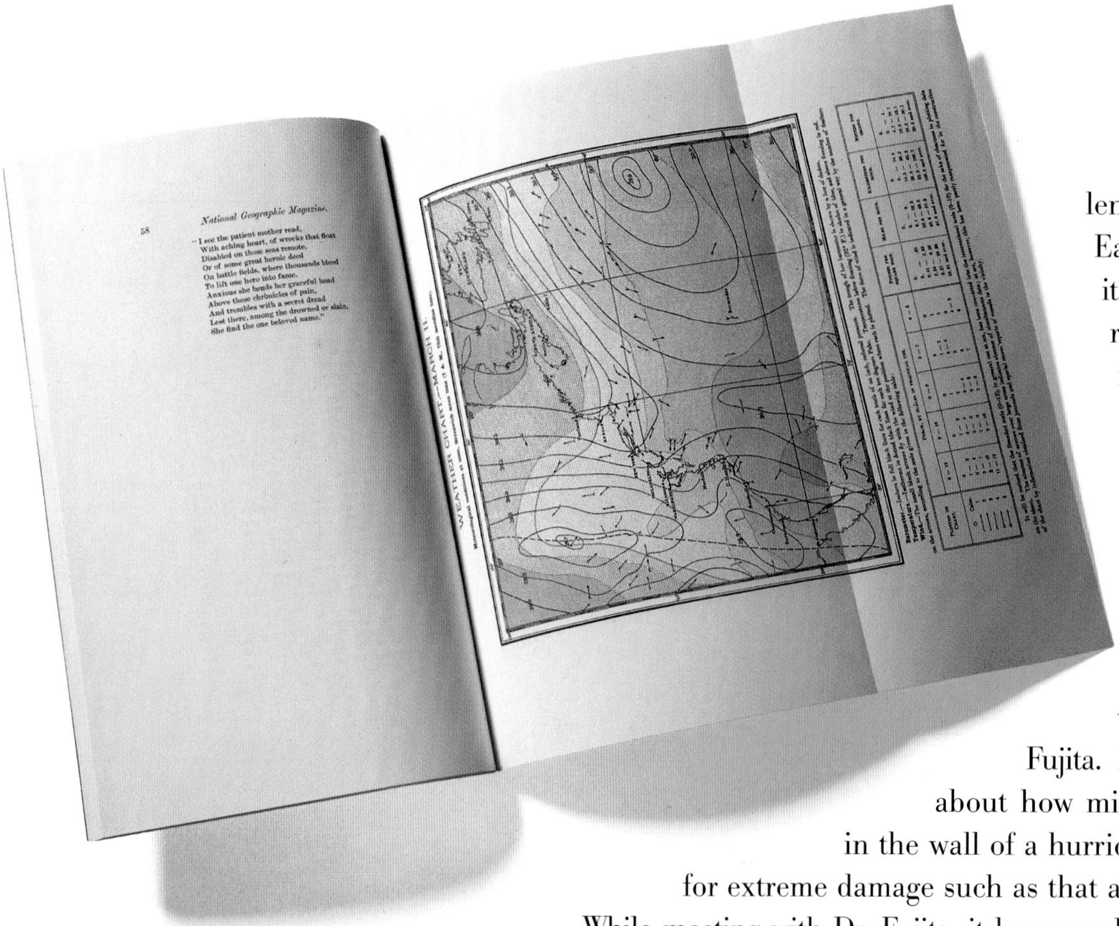

Figure 2: NATIONAL GEOGRAPHIC'S first diagram appeared in its maiden issue of October 1888.

lengths to ensure accuracy. Each Society publication, be it a magazine, book, or atlas, represents an extraordinary effort to that end.

This effort sometimes includes significant amounts of travel. For the Hurricane Andrew diagram I had to fly from Washington, D.C., to Chicago to meet with tornado expert Dr. Ted Fujita. Fujita had a new theory about how mini-tornadoes that formed in the wall of a hurricane could be responsible for extreme damage such as that at Pinewood Village.

While meeting with Dr. Fujita, it became clear that I needed to go to Florida to get more information from scientists at the National Hurricane Center, as well as to see the damage for myself.

The diagram took three months to complete. That was extremely fast for us and was possible only because we put aside everything else, but it is a timetable that many diagram artists would envy—particularly those working on newspapers. One of our art directors at the time, Mark Holmes, had been a newspaper diagram artist. He once calculated that the minimum amount of time it took to prepare artwork for NATIONAL GEOGRAPHIC was seven months. A normal schedule would take as long as a year.

Holmes says when he came to work for the magazine he experienced a culture shock. "We used to crank out two or three diagrams a night at the newspaper. It was like being in a M.A.S.H. unit. It didn't matter much how the graphic got done as long as it got done. At the GEOGRAPHIC, how you get there is as important as what gets there."

Absent the immediacy of a typical news magazine's deadlines, the NATIONAL GEOGRAPHIC is able to devote a great deal of time to each story, with the result that an article often becomes a definitive account of an event. The enormous print run is another time-consuming factor. It takes the printing plant in Mississippi an entire month—running day and night—to print all nine million copies of one issue. Artwork for the magazine needs to be ready for the printers almost half a year before the issue date because it has to go through many stages of proof to ensure the highest level of quality and accuracy.

A Parade of Diagrams

When NATIONAL GEOGRAPHIC magazine was born in 1888, it was a scientific journal. Gilbert H. Grosvenor, who became the magazine's Editor in 1903, slowly transformed the publication into something more. He envisioned a magazine that straddled the gap that separates the scientist from the lay reader. His formula was an un-flinching devotion to accuracy—required by the scientific commu-nity—and an equal commitment to lively photographic and artis-tic illustration, which made the magazine appealing to an infor-mation-hungry public.

Figure 3: Artist Hashime Murayama created an innovative diagram for an article on beetles.

The first diagram ap-peared in the magazine's maiden issue of October 1888. A particularly nasty winter storm had struck the northeastern U.S. and meteorologist Everett Hayden took it upon himself to write "The Great Storm of March 11-14, 1888." He chose to include a diagram showing the dramatic drop in barometric pressure recorded during the storm from different weather stations and vessels (Figure 2).

It took artist Hashime Murayama to raise diagrams in the magazine to another level. In the 1920s, he explored ways to make information graphics dynamic and visually compelling. Grosvenor recognized Murayama's impressive talent. Until Murayama's time, the expensive process of reproducing images in color had been reserved for photography and paintings. Now, diagrams were able to increase in size as well as appear in color.

Murayama's relationship with NATIONAL GEOGRAPHIC lasted two decades. During that time he illustrated a parade of diagrams and natural history subjects. Murayama introduced graphic approaches to diagrams that the magazine's artists still use today. In his diagram of the life cycle of a Japanese beetle (Figure 3), for example, he employed both what we call a "cutaway" and a "zoom." In a cutaway the artist removes a portion of the earth or a building to show what is underneath. A zoom magnifies an area. The same diagram presents a step-by-step life cycle of the beetle, another device we still use today.

In the 1960s, a team of new artists brightened the pages of NATIONAL GEOGRAPHIC. Their mark was big, bold, beautifully drawn graphics on timely subjects like pollution, astronomy, oceanography, and the space effort. They received commissions as part of an impressive shift in the look of the magazine, engineered by the magazine's new Editor, Melville Bell Grosvenor.

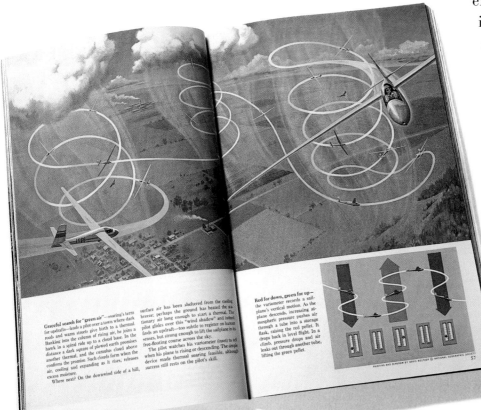

Figure 4: A lyrical illustration of gliding from the 1960s shows the large, colorful diagram displays that became the norm for NATIONAL GEOGRAPHIC.

Reflecting on his experience redesigning the magazine, then Art Director Howard Paine says: "The Editor led us into a world of new subjects that had to be illustrated in new ways, not as a quiet series of paintings, but as cutaways, exploded views, and gatefolds." This magazine, with a new look and new artists, was the NATIONAL GEOGRAPHIC that my generation—the baby boomers—grew up with. Subject by subject, our knowledge of the world expanded as we read the magazine and the Society's books. Our visual literacy was being shaped by brilliant color photography and illustrations.

Take, for example, Meltzer's 1967 diagram of a glider (Figure 4). The artist leads us smoothly through the spirals of glider flight. We intuitively understand what the diagram is about without explanation. We become interested in the subject simply because it is fun to look at. That was the secret of the new diagrams. They were so interesting—and entertaining—we learned to expect nothing less. From Jacques Cousteau to the Leakeys, from Mercury to Gemini and Apollo, visual inspiration from the scientific world surrounded us.

The NATIONAL GEOGRAPHIC I grew up with not only let one see into these worlds of science but also reflected the scientific understanding of that time. This has been true for every decade of the magazine's history. From 1919, for example, a diagram illustrating the solar system displays the scientific understanding of celestial mechanics. But Pluto is missing. The planet wasn't discovered until 1930. A diagram from 1946 illustrates our early exploration of the atmosphere. The highest flight by an airplane features a biplane. An unmanned rocket had reached to 75 miles. An ominous label placed at the 15-mile-high mark, reflecting the trepidation with which humans were probing this new domain, simply states, "Human blood boils."

The diagrams in the magazine have kept pace with science and the rapidly expanding visual literacy of the reading public. New artists commissioned over the years—especially since the 1960s—have kept the diagrams fresh and contemporary. The majority of artwork appearing in this collection of the Society's diagrams is from the last 25 years.

Selecting diagrams for inclusion in this book was not difficult. They stood out for their clarity and beauty, qualities that are never separate in a good diagram. These illustrations provide evidence of how the best art can proudly stand alongside the best photography in NATIONAL GEOGRAPHIC.

PART I

Beneath the Surface

In preparing his master plan for the dome of St. Peter's, Michelangelo built intricate clay models and sliced away sections to illustrate the beauty of the interior design. Like Michelangelo's dome, the artwork in this section belies the saying that beauty is only skin deep. Peeling away layers reveals the beauty that lies inside walls of stone, steel, and skin. With surgeons' skill, NATIONAL GEOGRAPHIC diagram artists slice into cathedrals, boats, and even the human brain to uncover their hidden structures.

As flexible as they are talented, these artists do not shrink from the challenge of tackling diverse subjects. Dale Gustafson, for example, is as comfortable illustrating a nuclear submarine as he is drawing a potato. Ed Gazsi deftly handles a see-through diagram of the human body to explore the effects of alcohol. Using his paintbrush as a can opener, staff artist Chris Klein pries open a tarantula, a horseshoe crab, and then a volcano. It's human nature to be curious about what's on the inside of things. These diagrams provide us with fantastic X-ray vision. Perhaps that is why they are so intriguing to look at.

NR-1 EXPLORES THE OCEAN
Illustration by DALE GUSTAFSON

Wealthy cargo ships lost at sea during the Roman era used to be out of sight, out of reach, but never out of mind for archaeologists. Teamed with scientific and technical pioneers led by Robert D. Ballard, archaeologists retrieved and studied artifacts from as deep as 2,800 feet in the Mediterranean Sea with the aid of a once-secret U.S. Navy nuclear research submarine NR-1.

Ballard writes: "During four explorations beginning in 1988 our Skerkie Bank Deep Sea Project documented eight ships: five Roman wrecks dating from about 100 B.C to A.D. 400, one 17th- or 18th-century wreck of North African origin, and two from the 19th or 20th centuries. All were within a 55-square-mile area." A textblock on the art reads: "A nuclear reactor as small as a garbage can allows NR-1 to prowl indefinitely without surfacing. The sub's deep-sea capability and equipment enable scientists to locate sites for further exploration with *Jason* (the remote operating vehicle equipped with cameras, sonar, and mapping and retrieving capabilities). At one stretch they were finding a wreck every other day."

Illustrator Dale Gustafson and art director Jeff Osborne captured the atmosphere of deep sea exploration with a black background and green light. Illuminating the key components of the ship and its prize discoveries gives a look inside, while retaining the realism of the image.

NATIONAL GEOGRAPHIC—April 1998

Nuclear reactor
compartment

Steel pressure hull,
1.3 inches thick

TV and
still cameras

Side-scanning
sonar

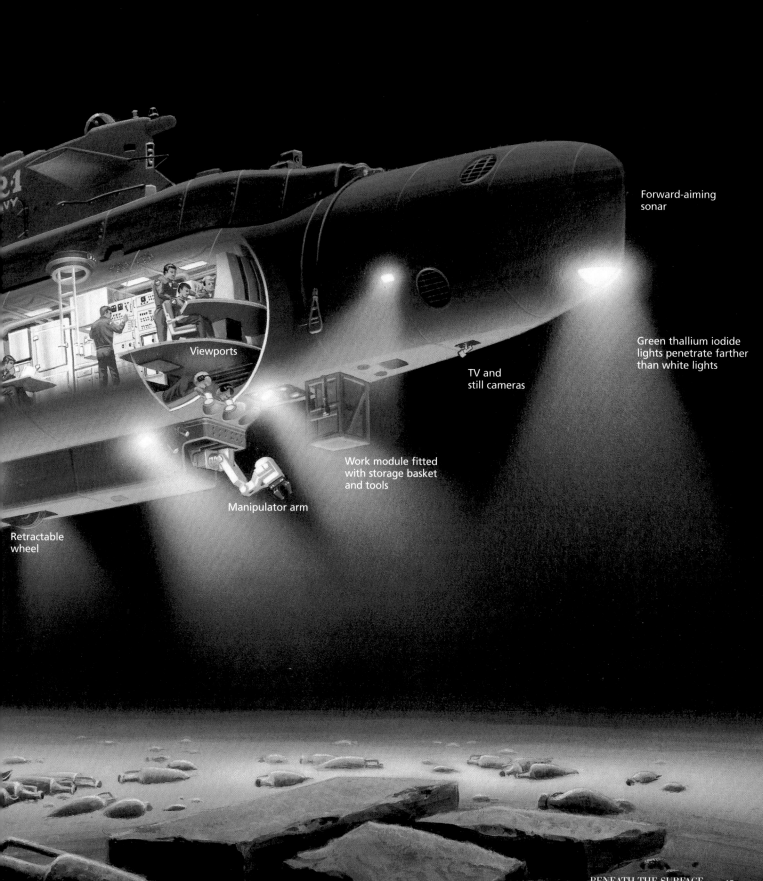

Forward-aiming
sonar

Green thallium iodide
lights penetrate farther
than white lights

Viewports

TV and
still cameras

Work module fitted
with storage basket
and tools

Manipulator arm

Retractable
wheel

TARANTULAS
Illustration by CHRISTOPHER A. KLEIN

For months, a jar labeled *Theraphosa blondi* and containing a pickled tarantula was the talk of visitors to room 870 at NATIONAL GEOGRAPHIC headquarters. Staff artist Chris Klein often shares his office with peculiar critters. This spider was part of the artist's reference material provided by art researcher Darcy Bellido de Luna and tarantula expert Rick West. The jar provided safe, close-up, and three-dimensional observation of the anatomy of a timid and generally misunderstood arachnid.

Klein's painting, which removes part of the carapace, is color-coded to allow easier viewing of the tarantula's innards: "four lungs (blue), primitive heart (magenta), nervous system (yellow), digestive tract (green), egg sac (beige), and silk-producing glands (purple)," explained the published text.

Author Richard Conniff, whose self-described "interest in animals humans commonly deem loathsome" led to this assignment on tarantulas, reports on the spider's mating technique, diagnosis and treatment of arachnophobia, and hunting tarantulas for profit. Photographs show the hairy tarantula buoyantly skipping across water, slipping into its silk-tree home, and squeezing out of its outgrown skin. Klein's diagram provides the story's only peek inside the tarantula to show how the spider functions.

NATIONAL GEOGRAPHIC—September 1996

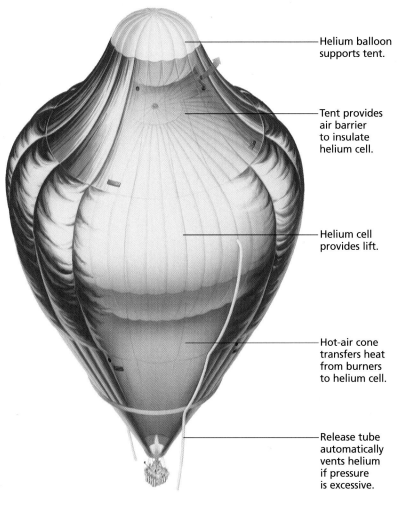

Helium balloon
supports tent.

Tent provides
air barrier
to insulate
helium cell.

Helium cell
provides lift.

Hot-air cone
transfers heat
from burners
to helium cell.

Release tube
automatically
vents helium
if pressure
is excessive.

MECHANICS OF
RACING WITH THE WIND
Illustrations by DALE GUSTAFSON

Author Richard Conniff calls it "the century's last great aeronautical prize: first around the world nonstop in a balloon." Pilot Steve Fossett dreamed of winning first place, but two other teams also took the risks and found the funding for attempts in 1997. None of the three teams made it, but all plan to try again.

Illustrator Dale Gustafson's diagram explains the mechanics of Fossett's balloon, *Solo Spirit.* Categorized as a Rozière, the balloon design includes a helium cell inside an envelope of hot air, with a smaller helium balloon supporting a tent that shields the main helium cell from the sun. The Rozière model addresses the basic problem in ballooning: overheating in the day and overcooling in the night.

Jean-Francois Pilatre de Rozière, after whom the balloon design was named, was one of the the first men to fly a balloon—in November 1783. As Conniff reports, "De Rozière's ingenious idea was to combine the maneuverability of hot air with the buoyancy of gas for an attempt to cross the English Channel in 1785. But the gas he used was hydrogen, and he died in a fiery plunge from 1,600 feet high. The modern Rozière balloon, introduced 20 years ago, uses nonflammable helium."

The National Geographic Society has a long and proud history of supporting balloonists who seek new records. A time line in the 1997 article states that "in November 1935, NGS and the U.S. Army sponsored *Explorer II*, which lifted two airmen and more than two tons of equipment 72,395 feet—a record that stood for 21 years."

NATIONAL GEOGRAPHIC—September 1997

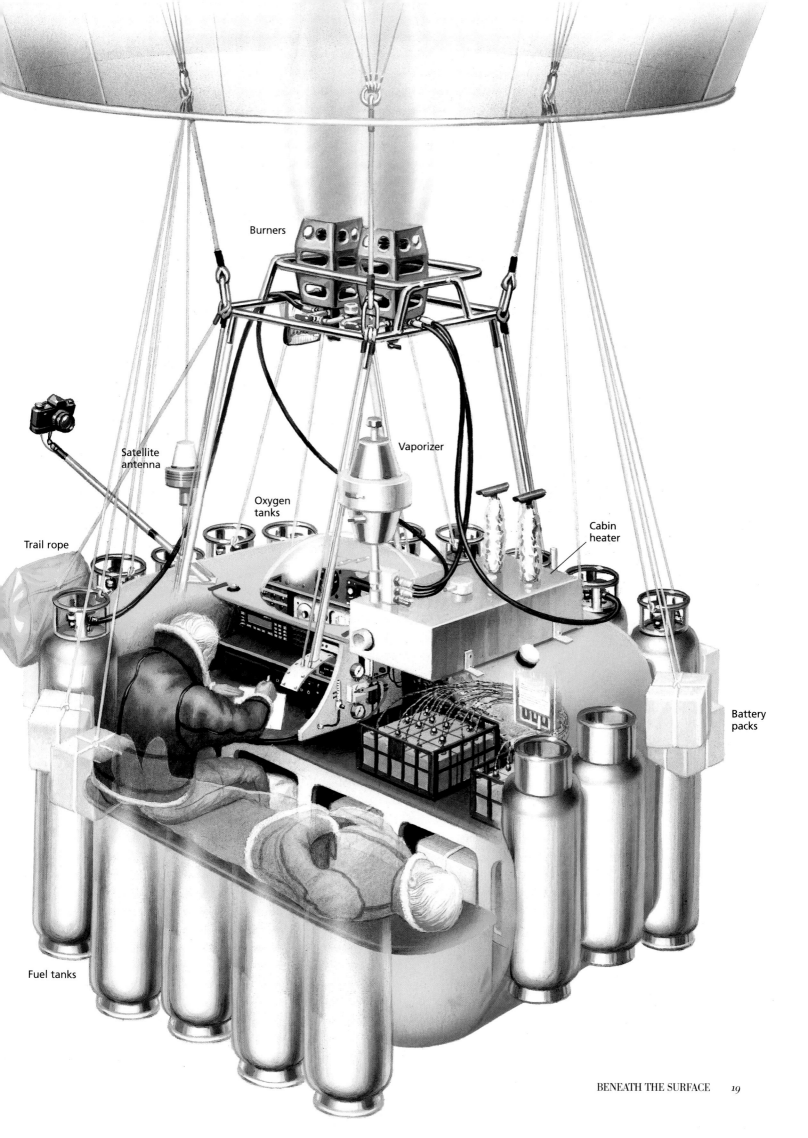

Burners

Vaporizer

Satellite
antenna

Cabin
heater

Oxygen
tanks

Trail rope

Battery
packs

Fuel tanks

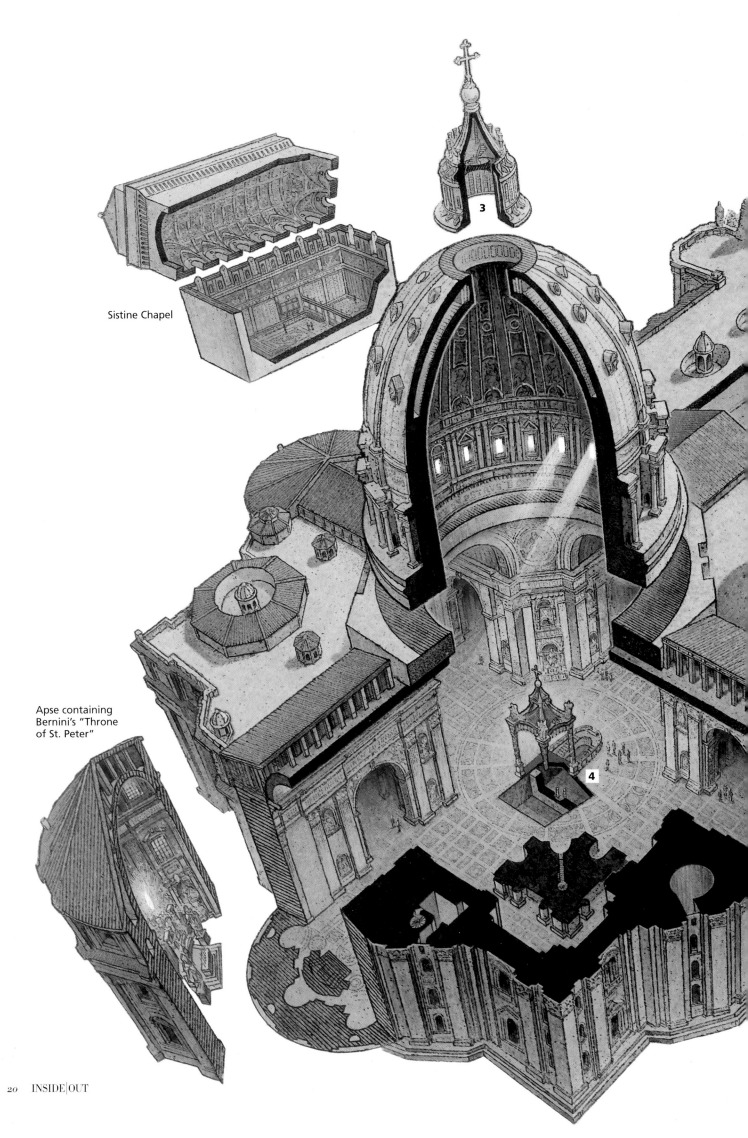

Sistine Chapel

Apse containing
Bernini's "Throne
of St. Peter"

3

4

THE VATICAN
Illustration by **HARRY BLISS**

Text accompanying this 1985 diagram of St. Peter's Basilica and Piazza in Vatican City gives the diagram historical context and architectural scale:

"On the bones of St. Peter—tradition holds—the world's largest church took shape in the hands of Italy's great Renaissance and Baroque artists. Consecrated in 1626 after more than a century of planning and building, it replaced the first St. Peter's Basilica, raised by the Christian Roman Emperor Constantine in the early fourth century.

"Nearly 700 feet long and 450 feet wide, the travertine-stone church can hold 50,000 worshippers. On the holiest days, nearly a quarter of a million people gather in the piazza (1), designed by Gian Lorenzo Bernini in the mid-17th century. A cross symbolizing the triumph of Christianity tops an 82-foot-high Egyptian obelisk (2), moved here in 1586 from the site of the Roman circus where St. Peter is believed to have been crucified around A.D. 65.

"More than 400 feet high, a lantern tower (3) crowns Michelangelo's incomparable dome. The tower centers above the now subterranean shrine (4) that was venerated by early Christians as St. Peter's burial place. The grave lies behind and below the mosaic of Christ illuminated in the confessio, or tomb of a martyr, a floor below the high altar. Bernini created the altar's towering bronze baldachin, along with much of the basilica's breathtaking interior decoration."

Art director Bob Teringo and illustrator Harry Bliss designed the page to partner with the previous magazine spread, which showed a modern aerial photograph and street map. The diagram simplifies the complex architecture by taking the site out of context and looking beneath the stone walls and mosaic floor. An emphasis on architectural splendor is the result. Bliss's perspective drawing skills and ink-and-wash medium created a lasting reference for tourists, history buffs, and art students.

NATIONAL GEOGRAPHIC—December 1985

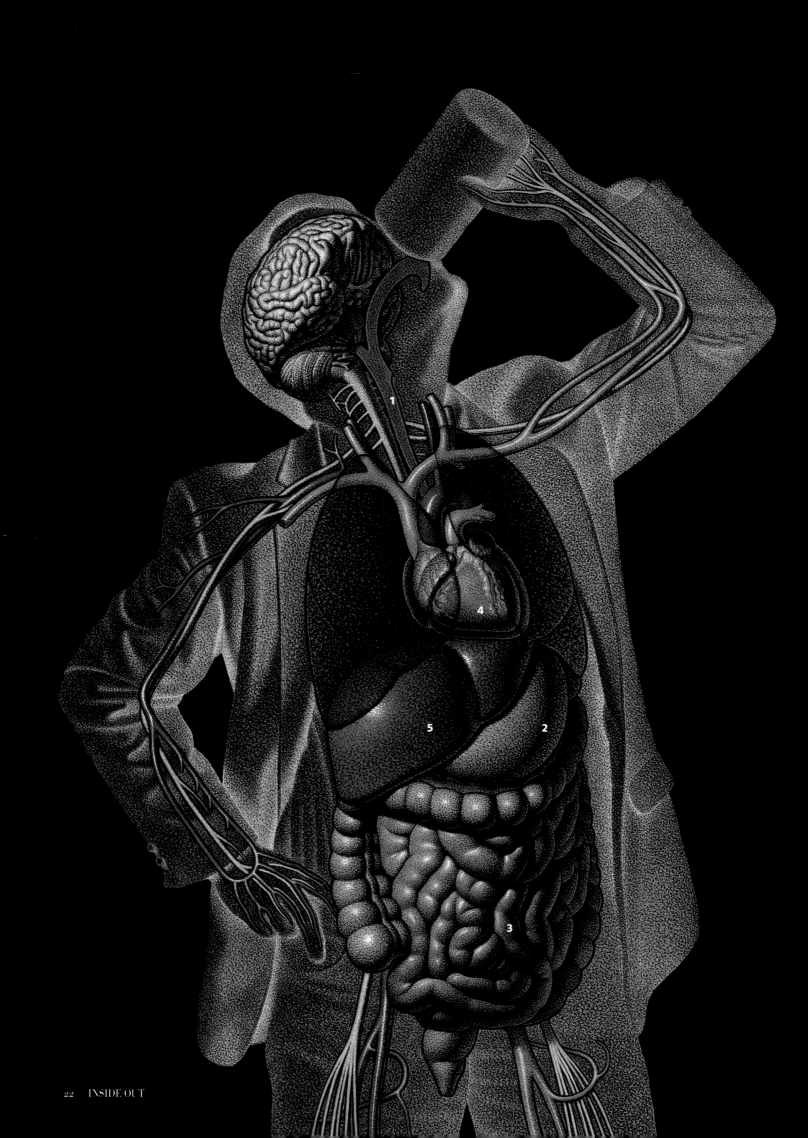

WHAT HAPPENS WHEN YOU DRINK

Illustration by EDWARD S. GAZSI

Bellying up to the bar might not be so popular a pastime if this visible man were the bartender.

The body organs involved in the processing of alcohol are illustrated by Ed Gazsi in a ghosted image of a suited drinker. Paraphrasing from the published caption: "1) The mouth and esophagus are briefly irritated by the first taste of alcohol. 2) The stomach absorbs some alcohol, but passes it on to (3) the small intestine, where it is moves rapidly into the bloodstream. The heart (4) can be aided against coronary heart disease by alcohol in moderation, but heavy drinking can lead to muscle tissue damage. 5) The liver metabolizes alcohol using enzymes that convert ethanol into carbon dioxide and water. Pure alcohol is metabolized by the liver at the rate of one-third ounce per hour."

Photography and text for this story covered the social effects and integration of alcohol in world cultures. The science, industry, and business of alcohol were also photographed. Only a diagram could illustrate the mechanics of alcohol's journey through the human body from the lips to the liver.

NATIONAL GEOGRAPHIC—February 1992

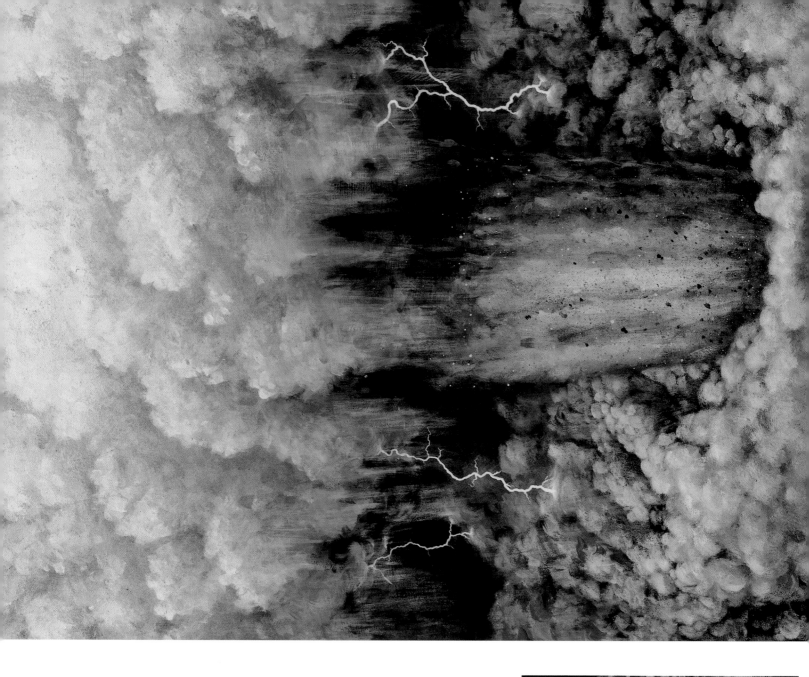

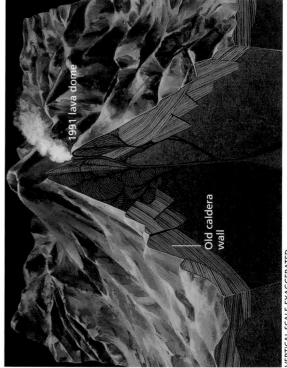

1991 lava dome

Old caldera wall

VERTICAL SCALE EXAGGERATED

Pyroclastic
flow

Magma chamber

PINATUBO: READY TO BLOW WITH THE BIG BLOW

Illustrations by WILLIAM H. BOND *and* CHRISTOPHER A. KLEIN

Mount Pinatubo decided 600 years of silence was long enough. Hinting impatiently at the violence it would cause to central Luzon in the Philippines, the volcano rumbled in April 1991 with vigorous steam eruptions, shallow earthquakes, sulfur dioxide emissions, and a rapidly growing lava dome. Nearby villages were evacuated when vigilant scientists, using monitoring instruments, noted the changes. Explosions began on June 12.

The story was about volcanoes around the world, but Pinatubo was the most recent explosion. Staff artist Bill Bond illustrated how volcanoes cause such powerful devastation, using both a generic model and Mount Pinatubo's specific case.

Page design, by art director Mark Holmes, assisted in the explanation. The gatefold—a third page (above) folded over the top of the painting—shows Mount Pinatubo in cross-section prior to its June eruption. Opened out, the gatefold illustrates the blast, with black sky filled with ash and pumice. Pyroclastic flows, 1,500°F and released when lava domes cave in, are indicated with arrows. Below ground level, the magma chamber glows a fiery red.

Bond built a scale model of Mount Pinatubo to visualize both the outside and the inside of the volcano. Using a detailed topographic map, he cut foam core layers following the contour lines and covered the layers with modeling clay. Like cutting a slice of cake, he cut the mountain model to form the base of this view.

It would have been artistically convenient for Mount Pinatubo to be a large and dramatic mountain, but it was small. Bond chose a common cartographic trick and exaggerated the vertical scale, careful to note the change in the caption.

Bond's precise method of modeling built him a reputation in the office for accurate and visually interesting illustrations. At home, though, where he builds the models, he finds his house taken over by landforms like Pinatubo, the Four Corners, and the Russian Steppes.

NATIONAL GEOGRAPHIC—December 1992

THE HEALTHY BRAIN
Illustration by KEITH KASNOT

"Infinitely more complex than any machine ever invented, the brain is the essence of what makes us human. Its blood vessels nourish three pounds of delicate tissue. Its billions of cells mysteriously regulate the body, learn from a lifetime of experiences, and summon the memories and thoughts unique to each of us," writes Joel Swerdlow, introducing the story on the human brain.

Photographs and text for the article highlight recent research in understanding the brain's role in facilitation of learning, motor-skill development and loss, reflex control, and illness. The diagram shown here serves as a visual glossary and reference tool for subjects covered in words and pictures.

As the published caption states: "Recent developments in imaging have improved our view of the architecture and workings of the brain. Each of its hemispheres, right and left, controls the opposite side of the body. Regions within a hemisphere specialize in certain functions— the motor cortex, for instance, helps control conscious movement.... Neurons send and receive electrochemical signals in mere thousandths of a second at connection points called synapses."

Designed to show normal, healthy brain functioning, this diagram was published as a gatefold illustration. When unfolded, the diagram showed the abnormal, unhealthy brain as confused by stroke, Alzheimer's disease, and schizophrenia. The clever design was the brainchild of former art director Mark Holmes, who moved on to become editor of National Geographic Interactive.

"The design of this brain diagram reflects my growing interest at that time in how readers interact with visuals," Holmes explained. Certified medical illustrator Keith Kasnot, with an expertise in medical and anatomical drawing, was able to interpret complex information for a general audience.

NATIONAL GEOGRAPHIC—June 1995

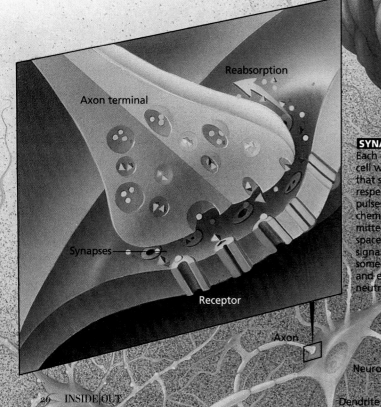

Motor cortex

Cortex

Ventricles

Amygdala

Hippocampus

Limbic system

SYNAPSE
Each neuron is a single nerve cell with axons and dendrites that send or receive signals respectively. When a signal pulses to the end of an axon, chemicals called neurotransmitters cross the minute space, or synapse. To end the signal, the axon reabsorbs some neurotransmitters, and enzymes in the synapse neutralize others.

Reabsorption

Axon terminal

Synapses

Receptor

Axon

Neuron

Dendrite

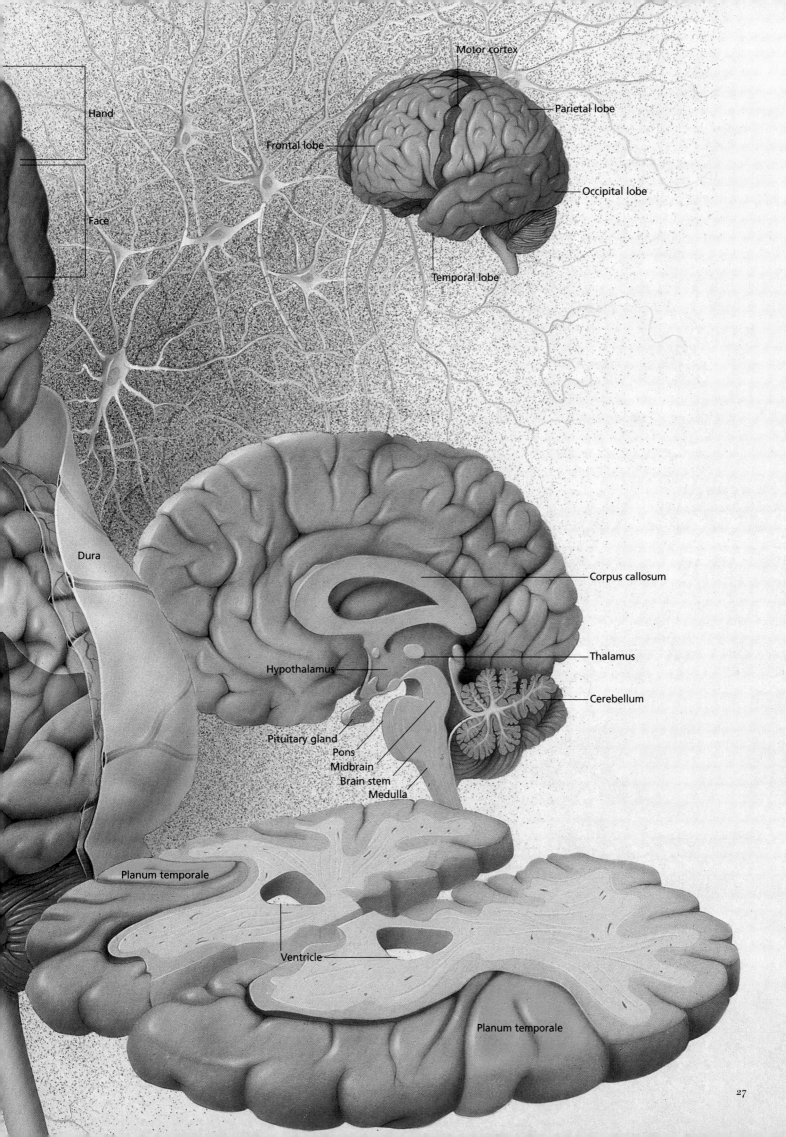

Hand

Face

Motor cortex

Frontal lobe

Parietal lobe

Occipital lobe

Temporal lobe

Dura

Corpus callosum

Hypothalamus

Thalamus

Cerebellum

Pituitary gland

Pons

Midbrain

Brain stem

Medulla

Planum temporale

Ventricle

Planum temporale

27

THE NOBLE POTATO

Illustration by DALE GUSTAFSON

Appealing in every way, the potato is produced in more countries than any other crop, except corn. Eight species are cultivated, with more than 5,000 varieties. As the published caption states: "Rootlike, and often mislabeled accordingly, the potato is actually a tuber, part of the underground stem. The plant sprouts from an eye, or bud, of a sown potato piece."

Neatly sliced to graphically represent usage, *Solanum tuberosum*—the only potato species grown in the United States—is shown to be consumed largely fresh (32% of the 16-million-ton U.S. harvest) or French fried and frozen (27%).

This diagram, a personal favorite of *Inside/Out* project director David Griffin because of its informative yet whimsical style, was artist Dale Gustafson's first assignment for the Society. A hint at his knack for high-tech illustration (see NR-1, pages.14-15) gleams in the metallic potato peeler, almost a sculpture in itself. The illustration, overseen by art director Jan Adkins, also marked the beginning of similar "sliced produce" diagrams in other stories on commodities such as corn (June 1993).

NATIONAL GEOGRAPHIC—May 1982

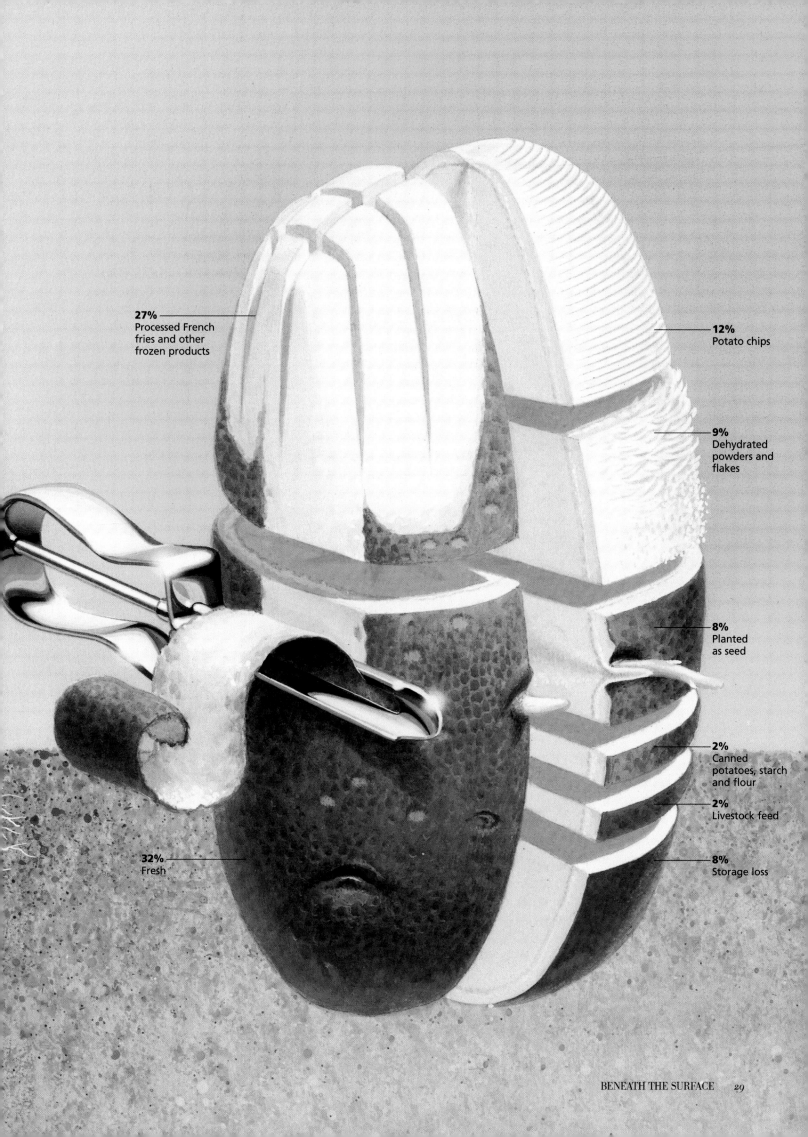

27%
Processed French
fries and other
frozen products

12%
Potato chips

9%
Dehydrated
powders and
flakes

8%
Planted
as seed

2%
Canned
potatoes, starch
and flour

2%
Livestock feed

32%
Fresh

8%
Storage loss

ANCIENT MERCHANTS
Illustration by NED *and* ROSALIE SEIDLER

The arrival of a Syrian fleet laden with riches collected from all over the Mediterranean world would be cause for festivities in the 14th century B.C. But this celebration was delayed until 1982, when the sunken ship's cargo remains were discovered by a sponge diver in a sediment-rich area off the coast of Turkey.

A creative layout concept by art director Bob Teringo made this dramatic recreation possible. Split in half at the waterline, the ship was reconstructed reliably from archaeological evidence and precise site maps below the water. An Egyptian tomb painting from the same time period served as the base for the ship above the waterline.

Researchers led by NGS grantee Dr. George Bass at the Institute of Nautical Archaeology (INA) in Texas found hull planks fastened with mortise-and-tenon joints, "bronze swords and arrowheads, stone mace

heads, ostrich eggshells, ivory, and Mycenaean pottery. The hold at center stores fishing nets, blue glass ingots, logs of exotic wood, and amphorae filled with aromatic resin, flanked by storage jars. Copper and tin ingots are also stowed here, with more copper forward of the mast, where stone anchors are stacked in pairs. Atop the ballast stones the goods were cushioned by thorny burnet, a common Mediterranean shrub," describes the published caption.

Like photography of the time, artwork was detailed and straightforward. Skilled illustrators Ned and Rosalie Seidler provided the precision in light and shadow that makes a viewer want to reach out and touch the curvature of the amphorae. Part of a large department of staff artists at NGS during the years 1967 to 1985, Seidler's meticulous research and painting skills were well known. This piece by the Seidler husband-wife team is generally regarded as one of the finest illustrations the Society has published.

Photography and text for the article covered the discovery, the science of preservation, the Mediterranean trade, the landscape, and photographs of modern-day descendants of the people. The design, research, and precise execution of the diagram lent a seeing-is-believing authenticity to the report.

Archaeologists have credited NATIONAL GEOGRAPHIC diagrams with igniting their childhood curiosity in the very fields they have gone on to research. Peeking into the hold of this ancient ship laden with treasures may generate a few new students for INA.

NATIONAL GEOGRAPHIC—December 1987

SKYLAB
Illustration by ROBERT T. McCALL

With a dedication to exploration and discovery, NATIONAL GEOGRAPHIC has maintained steady reporting on the new frontier of space exploration. In the October 1974 issue of the magazine, Editor Gilbert M. Grosvenor committed an astounding 62 pages to the accomplishments of America's first manned orbiting laboratory.

In this diagram, Bob McCall cut away the side of Skylab, pride of the early 1970s space program, to reveal the inner workings. "As the mission unfolded, three successive crews of three astronauts each shuttled to the lab in Apollo spaceships. The first team occupied it for 28 days; the second, for 59; and the third, for

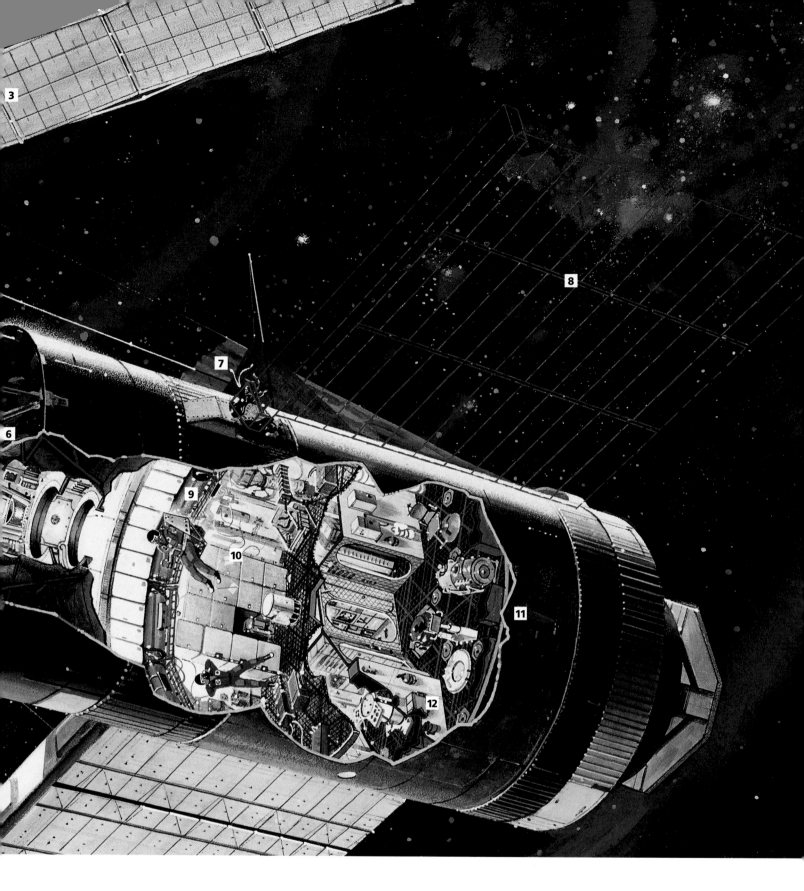

84 days. When the last team left the station on February 8, 1974, "Skylab had carried its crews 2,476 times around the globe—70 million miles—one of science's most productive journeys," wrote author Tom Canby.

The article was photographed by the astronauts themselves who had "mastered the art of maneuvering in zero gravity and delighted in televising their antics to earthlings," Canby wrote.

As the published caption reads: "Measuring 118 feet from stem to stern, Skylab carries the most varied assortment of experimental equipment ever assembled in a spacecraft. Her size and complexity became apparent in this artist's cutaway. 1) Command service module; 2) Apollo telescope mount; 3) ATM solar array; 4) Auxiliary docking port; 5) Multiple cocking adapter; 6) Airlock; 7) Sunshades; 8) Solar array (torn off during launch); 9) Water tanks; 10) Space maneuvering unit; 11) Orbital workshop; and 12) Wardroom."

The work done by Skylab, and the information it yielded, paved the way for the space shuttle program, heralded in NATIONAL GEOGRAPHIC in the 1980s.

NATIONAL GEOGRAPHIC—October 1974

TEKTITE II
Illustration by PIERRE MION

"Named after small glassy meteoric nodules found on ocean floors as well as on land, the Tektite project seeks to advance man's knowledge not only of the sea, but also of outer space and the best means of exploring it. Faced with the prospect of rotating crews on future space stations, NASA joined other government agencies in sponsoring the project. NASA's goal was to study the behavior of scientists working in rigid isolation," writes author John G. Vanderwalker. For seven months in 1970, a series of research teams—including an all-female group—lived 50 feet underwater.

Under the direction of the U.S. Department of the Interior, more than 40 American and foreign scientists joined this study of Great Lameshur Bay, off St. John in the U.S. Virgin Islands.

In this diagram, "members of the women's team (left) glide through gathering dusk toward the habitat, shown here in a detailed cutaway.... Another aquanaut (lower right) passes through a barred shark gate. An always open hatch leads up into the habitat, where air at two and a half times surface pressure holds back the sea. A diver towels off after a freshwater shower; above her, an air conditioner circulates the habitat's atmosphere of 9 percent oxygen and 91 percent nitrogen... Cylindrical tunnel leads to the control room. There the fifth aquanaut monitors communications and life-support systems. Below her are comfortable living quarters. On the seafloor, scientists studying the effects of grazing have set up a wire cage to protect plants from large fish," describes the published text.

Pierre Mion's diagram reflects the simple, upbeat, and almost cartoonlike style of the 1970s, which has since been supplanted by the 1990s style of virtual reality.

NATIONAL GEOGRAPHIC—August 1971

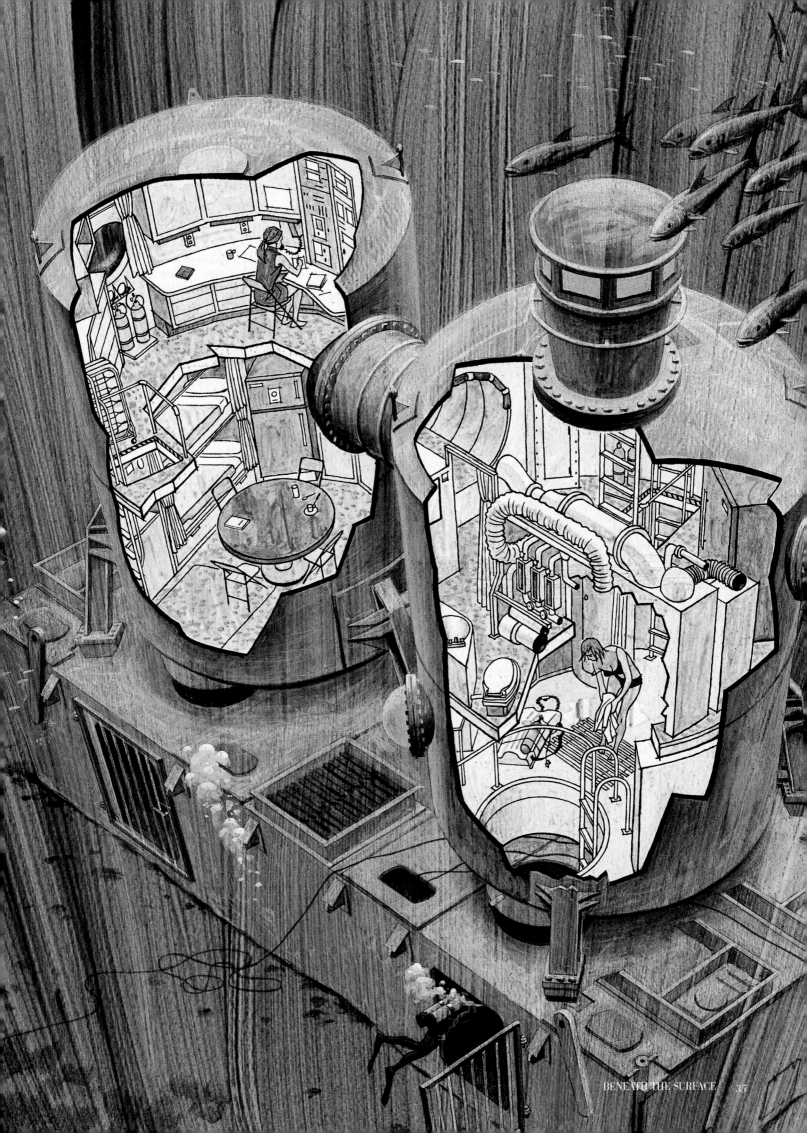

CATHEDRAL
Illustration by: HARRY BLISS

"Transcending earthly space, the Gothic cathedral soars heavenward.... Constructing these masterpieces of stone and glass with only the simple technology of medieval times required decades and the labor of hundreds. Gothic grace derived from an architectural combination of pointed arches, rib vaulting, and flying buttresses flanking the cathedral sides. Wooden frames supported the arched stone buttresses and vaulting until the cementing mortar dried. Throughout the finished interior, stained glass cast a multicolored spell. Magnificent rose windows often adorned the north, south, and west walls of the churches. Developing from the simpler wheel windows of the Romanesque, these Gothic jewels became more complex, as stained glass technology and Gothic architecture evolved," states the published text.

Illustrator Harry Bliss captured the busy construction site for a spread in a historical atlas entitled *Peoples and Places of the Past*, published in 1983 as a special project of the Society. Accompanying this cutaway was another, smaller diagram contrasting the dominant Romanesque style cathedral with the more graceful Gothic style.

Peoples and Places of the Past—1982

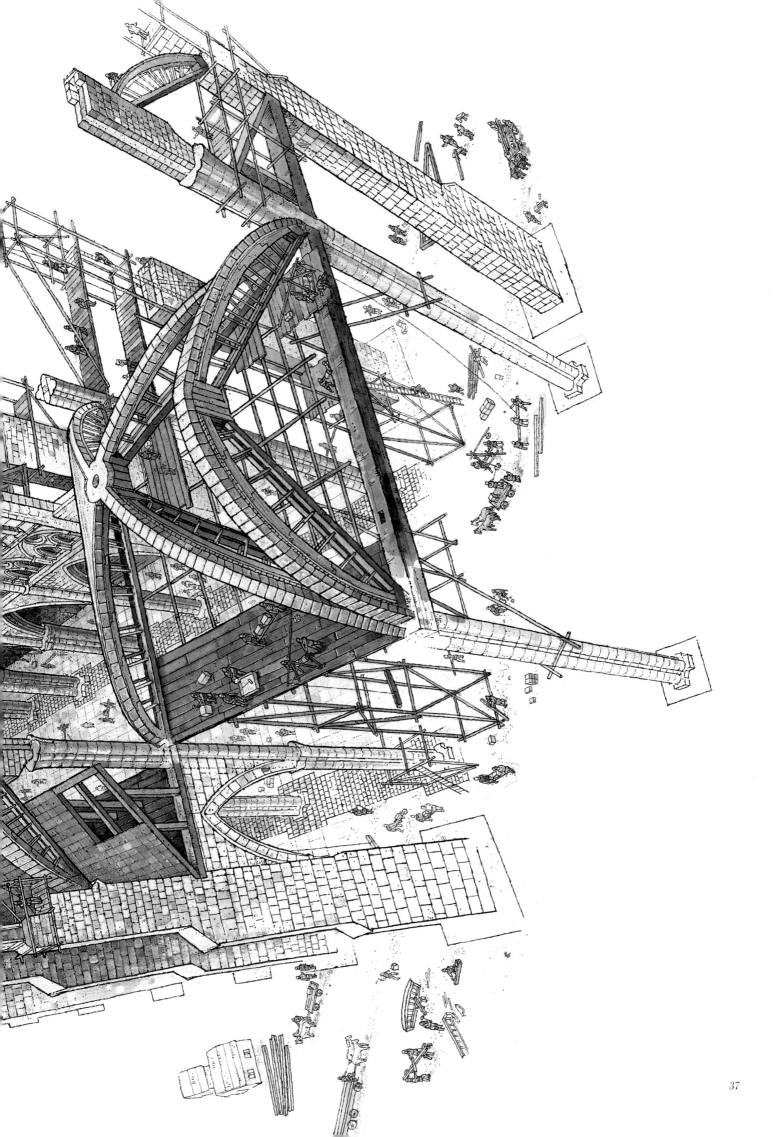

IN THE BELLY OF THE BEAST
Illustration by CHUCK CARTER

Eight years after the 1986 explosion of reactor No. 4 of the Chornobyl nuclear power plant, NATIONAL GEOGRAPHIC journalists revisited the area of the former Soviet Union contaminated by the worst nuclear disaster of all time.

Gerd Ludwig's photographs and Assistant Editor Mike Edwards's text document the devastating cost to human and environmental health in Ukraine, Belarus, and Russia. Understanding the unstable nature of the still-untamed nuclear monster required this diagram.

Artist Chuck Carter, whose computer-generated art became famous in the CD-ROM adventure-fantasy game *Myst*, was contracted to build a computer model of the reactor as a cutaway—to look inside the concrete and steel sarcophagus. So real was the rendering that when the editors viewed it with the pictures for the first time, they thought it was a photograph.

As the 1994 published caption states, "The rendering with the west wall cutaway reveals the reactor cavity of unit No. 4. It also shows how the reactor's ruined structure provides questionable physical support for the sarcophagus built around it. Four areas of the reactor are indicated:

"1) Sarcophagus—Since radiation was too hazardous for welders, the 246-foot-high structure was not hermetically sealed. More secure options have been studied, but cost too much for the near-bankrupt Ukrainian government.

"2) Water—Recycled for spraying to control immense amounts of radioactive dust inside the ruins, contaminated water—which increases with each rainfall seeping through the leaky roof—poses a growing threat to the groundwater below.

"3) Corium—Melted debris of the reactor core, corium was liquid during a short period of intense heat, then quickly solidified. Still warm from radioactive heat, it includes about 130 tons of uranium fuel and produces more radioactive dust as it degrades.

"4) Component E—The reactor's lid was blown askew by the explosion, its 2,000 tons of steel and concrete riddled with the pipes of broken fuel channels. Its counterpart shield under the core sank 13 feet in the blast."

Three days before the final art was due to the Engraving and Printing department, Carter lost the entire project when his computer's hard drive crashed. He and art director Mark Holmes completely rebuilt the art and met the deadline.

NATIONAL GEOGRAPHIC—August 1994

TALLGRASS PRAIRIE
Illustration by JOHN D. DAWSON

National Geographic published an article in August 1979 entitled, "Hard Life of the Prairie Dog." Exactly why the small mammals are eternally looking over their shoulders is revealed with a close look at this diagram of prairie life published 13 years later in a story on the American prairie. Text published with this diagram in 1993 describes the scene:

"More than a hundred species of vertebrates live around the prairie dog mounds that dot western shortgrass and mixed-grass prairie. Many come for a meal. Prairie dogs (1) are prey for badgers (2) and

occasionally weasels (3) and rattlesnakes (4). These invade burrows and may flush the rodents into the clutches of hawks (5) or stalking coyotes (6). A complex pattern of barks enables prairie dogs to warn of attacks (7) or signal an all clear (8).

"Their landscaping draws more benign company as well. Constant pruning of grasses such as blue grama (9) and little bluestem (10) spurs nutritious shoots that draw bison (11) and pronghorn (12). Vacant burrows house thirteen-lined ground squirrels (13) or prairie voles (14). Topside, western meadowlarks (15), upland

sandpipers (16), and lark buntings (17) compete for insects."

Artist John Dawson and his wife, Kathleen, who does research for his paintings, have freelanced for the Society for 16 years. John's first assignment—25 paintings for a story on ants—was published in 1984.

"Big, fat prairie dogs" from the National Zoo in Washington, D.C. —probably better fed than their relatives in the wild—modeled for the characters with the hard life in the foreground.

National Geographic—October 1993

MEDIEVAL CASTLE
Illustration by **HARRY BLISS**

A man might not want his home to be a castle when he takes a closer look through a castle's stone walls. Few modern home owners would care to replicate the cold, drafty rooms and foul odors a medieval castle contained. Few realtors would advertise a modern home for its military defense, the primary purpose of a feudal castle. "Location, location, location," however, is a common thread.

To summarize the text accompanying the art: Castle location allowed control of key terrain and communications and provided refuge. The earliest castles were little more than wooden watchtowers on high ground with protective stockades. Eventually, however, they evolved into strategic stone fortresses with thick walls, deep moats, and carefully engineered alignments and systems of observation and access. Their value as living quarters was secondary to their use as fortifications.

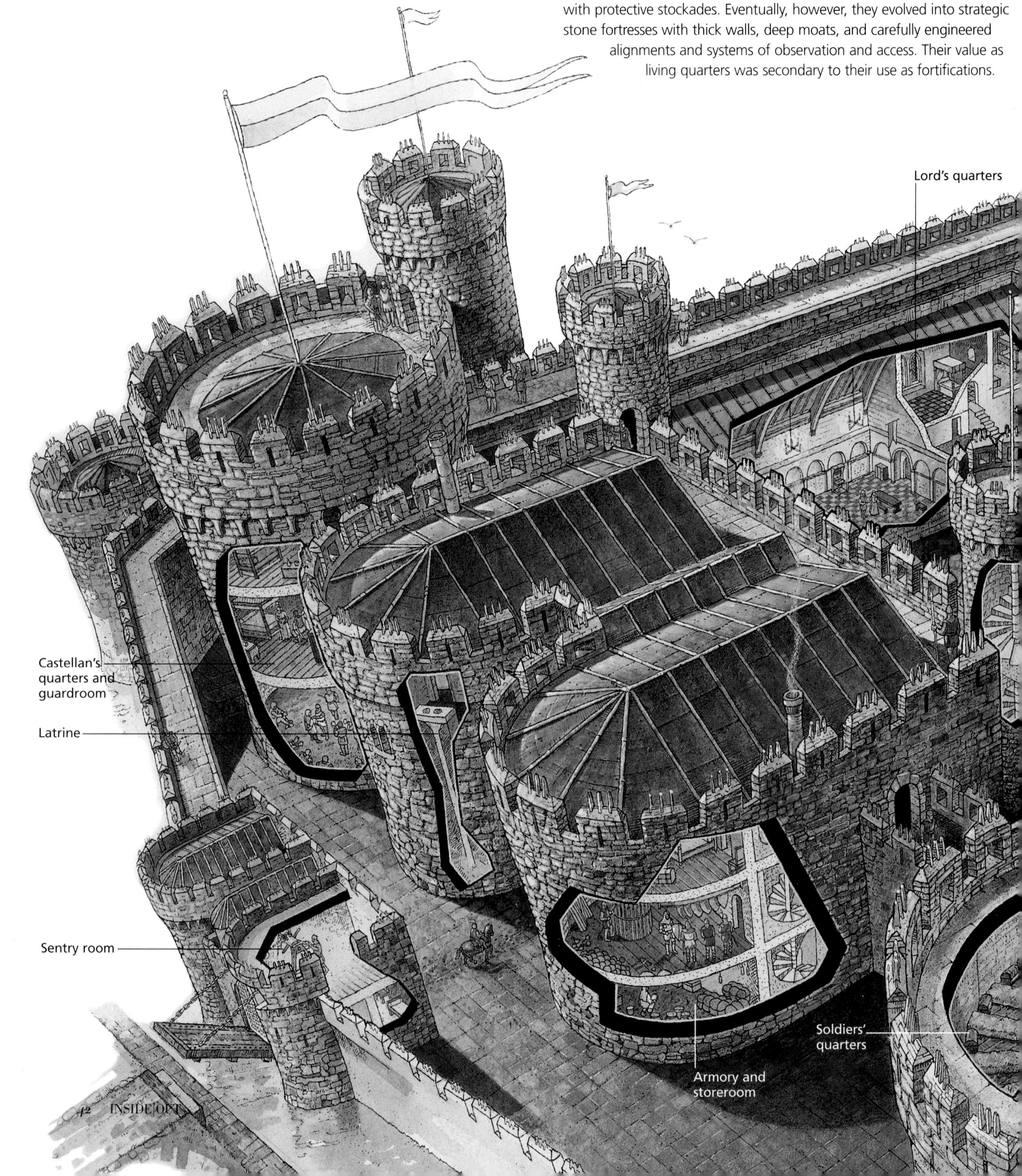

Lord's quarters

Castellan's quarters and guardroom

Latrine

Sentry room

Soldiers' quarters

Armory and storeroom

Feudalism was essentially a system of reciprocal agreements by which a lord granted possession of an estate, or fief, to a lesser noble in return for homage, loyalty, and military or political service. By subdividing their fiefs, the ruling nobility, over time, established the principle of hereditary use of the land.

Published in 1983, *Peoples and Places of the Past* was an atlas of major historical events, designed around maps, paintings, and diagrams. Since the theme was history, photographs were not the primary focus.

Art director Bob Teringo, on loan to the project from the magazine, designed a format in which each spread was a self-contained compilation of informative elements on a single topic. He hired freelance artists with varying, but complementary, styles and skills that brought life to history and geography. *Inside/Out* art director Suez Kehl, also on loan to this project from the Society's Book Division, took the layout to its final form.

Artist Harry Bliss painted this diagram for a chapter on Europe from A.D. 500 to 1500. Bliss's skill in perspective drawing (see Cathedral, pages 36-37) and clear style made the complexity of castle life easy to understand. So successful was his diagram that it was chosen to be a poster, with a reference time line, supplementing the book.

Peoples and Places of the Past—1983

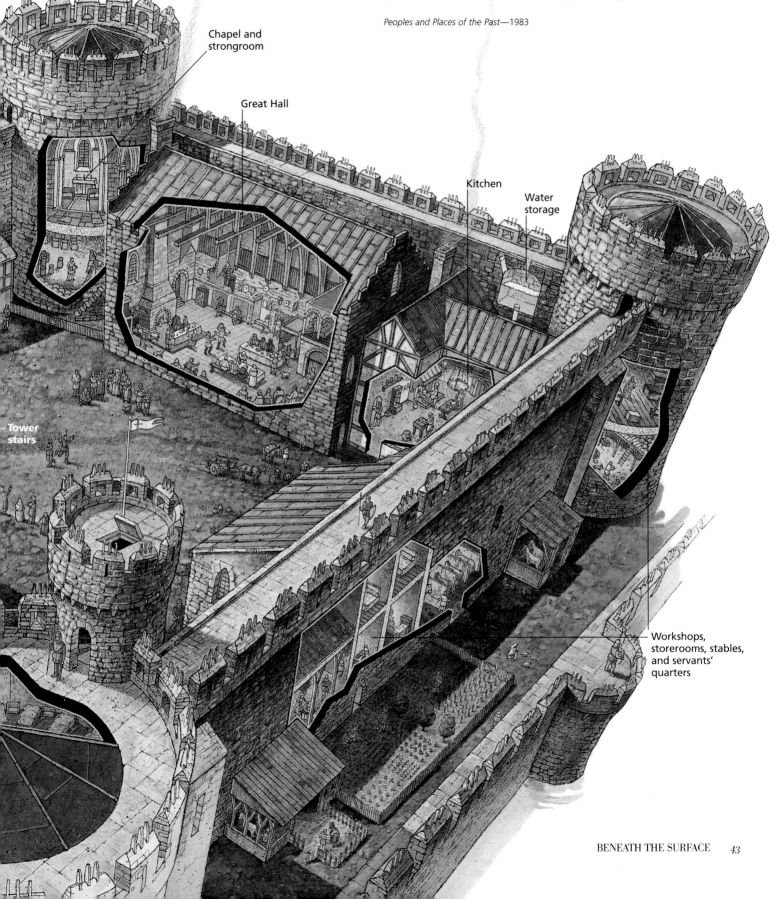

Chapel and strongroom

Great Hall

Kitchen

Water storage

Tower stairs

Workshops, storerooms, stables, and servants' quarters

FRESHWATER TURTLE
Illustration by **KAREL HAVLICEK**

Answering one of the most burning questions of childhood—what is inside a turtle?—this diagram explains the respiration, feet, shell, and growth of a red-eared slider (opposite).

Text on the published diagram explained the inner workings of a turtle. To paraphrase: In addition to breathing through a set of lungs, freshwater turtles can use their mouth cavity in gill-like fashion. Water is drawn through the nostrils, oxygen absorbed in the mouth cavity, and the water expelled.

Turtles apparently have keen eyesight and can distinguish colors, although they probably lack good long-distance vision. Old or ill turtles can go blind. The shell, in some species, is strong enough to resist an alligator's bite. Attached to the body by the backbone, the shell is not like a house—the turtle cannot walk out of it. Thick nails on the turtle's webbed feet come in handy for shredding food and digging in mud.

Czech-born illustrator Karel Havlicek achieves excellent detail by close observation and very sharp graphite and color pencils. This was his second assignment for the magazine. While illustrating the life of a tide pool for his first, he broke his hand in a car accident. The story was postponed, however, thereby permitting him to fulfill his lifelong dream to work for NATIONAL GEOGRAPHIC.

NATIONAL GEOGRAPHIC—January 1986

HORSESHOE CRAB
Illustration by **CHRISTOPHER A. KLEIN**

All field guides to Atlantic beaches should include artist Klein's cutaway painting of the primeval horseshoe crab. Beach walkers, long fascinated by those curious brown lumps-with-a-tail, would have a color-coded road map to the ancient species of ocean bottom dweller.

Shown here is *Limulus polyphemus*, one of four surviving species of horseshoe crabs with a range from Maine to Yucatan. Horseshoe crabs are misnamed—they are not crustaceans but are more closely related to spiders. By any name, horseshoe crabs were on earth before dinosaurs. The 1981 caption explains:

"In a view beneath its shell, major organs are color keyed: Curved gills in brown at rear, the elongated heart in red with the pericardial sac in blue, the tubular intestine and bulbous crop in green, and the gear-shaped brain in yellow. Five pairs of legs propel the bottom dweller, which feeds on worms and mollusks. In the water, the spike-like tail aids in maneuvering. When flipped upside down on the beach by the surf, the animal uses it like a lever in an effort to right itself."

Because it was a test assignment for NATIONAL GEOGRAPHIC, getting the details right was very important to now veteran artist Klein. "I didn't know what I was doing," he says. "All I could think was 'get it right and work for NATIONAL GEOGRAPHIC. Get it wrong and stay in sweatshops forever.'" The last night before it was due, he worked all night. "I heard the birds sing in the morning," he remembers.

NATIONAL GEOGRAPHIC—April 1981

MAYFLOWER
Illustration by RICHARD SCHLECHT

The celebrated *Mayflower* was actually a converted merchant ship, veteran of the French wine trade, and chartered in 1620 to carry colonists to "the Northerne parts of Virginia." A reconstruction of the ship, based on features common to others of her type, provided the information for this diagram.

"Dripping water chilled passengers in the tween-deck area (1). Cooking fires in the galley (2) were damped in rough weather. When high seas kept the beakhead (3) wet, latrine buckets were used. Fresh provisions stocked in the hold (4) had run out by November 11, when *Mayflower* anchored in Cape Cod Bay. The Mayflower Compact, probably signed in the 'great cabin' (5), established a design for self-government and protected the Pilgrims from legal challenge to settling north of their charter's limits," the published caption states.

Illustrator Richard Schlecht, whose journalism education, curious mind, and self-taught art skills drew him to the magazine, is noted for his expertise in drawing ships. Schlecht was assigned to this project in part because of his longtime collaboration with Ivor Nöel Hume, archaeologist at Colonial Williamsburg. Together, they developed authoritative visualizations of early American life.

Historical Atlas of the United States—1988

THE HUMAN BODY
Illustration by: **KIRK MOLDOFF**

"Known as the 'system of self,' the immune system possesses the remarkable ability to tell self from nonself, friend from foe. It recognizes and destroys cancer cells, transplanted tissue cells, and a wide range of organisms....," writes Jennifer Gorham Ackerman in *The Incredible Machine*, 1986.

The caption published with the art describes the immune system depicted: "Lymphatic vessels link the scattered organs of the immune system, shown in this diagram. A river of lymph sweeps dead cells and other debris through the channels, and dispatches white blood cells to battle infection. Lymph nodes cluster along the vessels, with major groups in the groin, abdomen, armpits, and neck. They filter the body's detritus."

The airbrush became a popular tool and technique that was especially effective for medical illustration. It enabled artists to achieve a realism similar to what a computer does for some of the more recent diagrams.

Art director David Seager and artist Kirk Moldoff meet the challenge of seeing beneath the surface of the human body into the lymphatic system, while retaining a sense of location within the body. The same base illustration was used elsewhere in the book for diagramming other internal body mechanisms. Layers of acetate on a single body outline indicated how various organs of the body operate. Seager credits the design inspiration for this diagram to the popular "visible body" diagrams he admired in the encyclopedia during his youth in the 1950s.

The Incredible Machine—1986

Adenoids

Tonsils

Thymus

Lymph node

Spleen

Peyer's patches (on small intestine)

Lymphatic vessels

Appendix

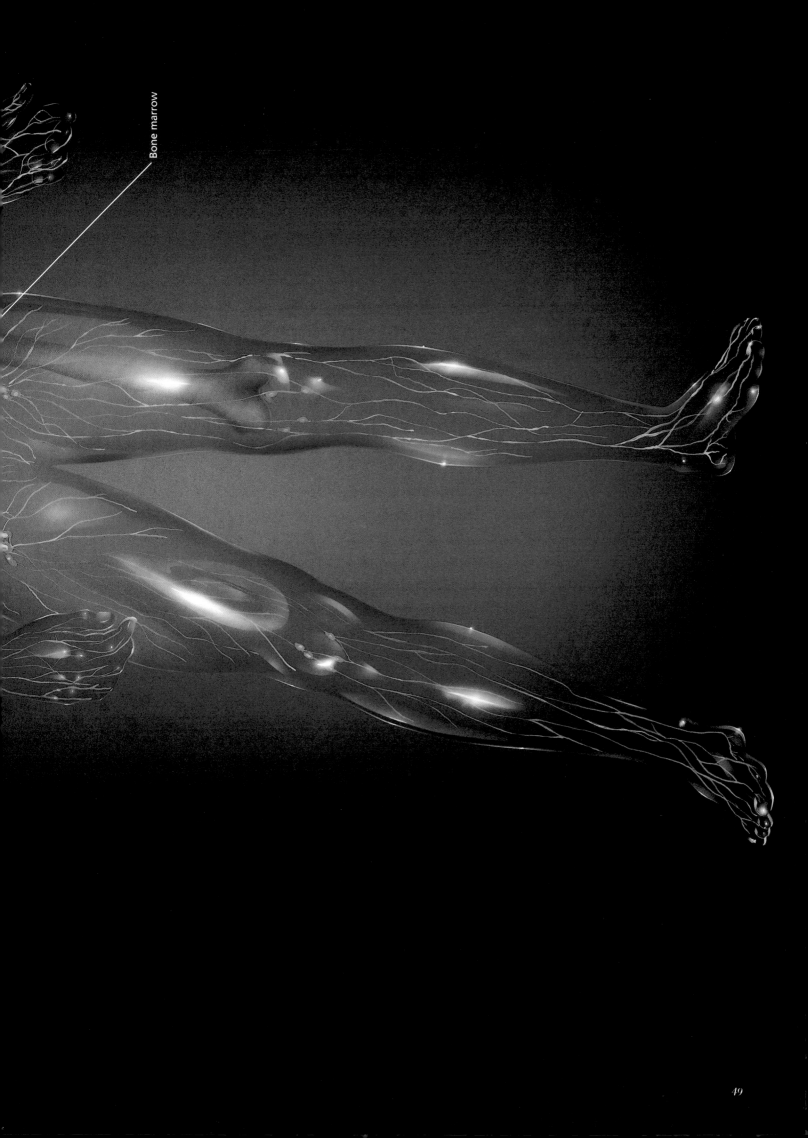

Bone marrow

A Digital Look Under New York

I N 1996, NATIONAL GEOGRAPHIC Art Director Allen Carroll, a true lover of diagrams, conceived a story called "Under New York" that would explore the complex web of subterranean utilities, transportation facilities, and other phenomena below street level. A large cutaway diagram was to be the centerpiece of the story.

Coincidentally, he had just received samples of computer graphics done by Don Foley, a former newspaper illustrator, now freelance, who was perfect for the job. When Carroll moved to the Society's map-making division I succeeded him as art director and became acquainted with Foley's work firsthand.

Foley started out with the first model of Apple Macintosh in the 1980s and has been riding the digital graphics wave ever since. On each of his jobs, he worked his machines hard. Every year new computers and new software made it possible to do more of his graphics on the computer. Foley kept up with it all, watching machines that he originally wouldn't even trust to draw a straight line evolve into truly formidable graphic allies.

When I started working on the story, art researcher Karen Gibbs had already pulled together a mass of information. She found an engineering firm—Vollmer Associates—with a contract to build a new subway station at 42nd and Broadway. It seemed like an ideal way to take a peek at what was under New York. The engineering firm had excellent subsurface information that they were willing to share.

Foley went to New York to meet with engineers from the firm. "They dragged me places other people couldn't go—probably because no one else would want to go there!" he says. He spent hours crawling in the dirt among pipes, wires, and rivets. Under the asphalt everything looked hopelessly entangled. The engineers hauled out plans to help the artist sort it all out. Drawings began to fill his sketchbook.

Foley was particularly intent on capturing details of different surface textures at the construction site, because he believes that attention to textures and lighting gives his models a realistic appearance. With this in mind he shot rolls of film of the site that included close-ups of tiles, bricks, dirt, and concrete.

A week after visiting New York, Foley sent in a carefully drawn pencil sketch. This surprised me because I had been expecting a computer image. "I find it's not a good idea to work on the computer when you're developing a concept. The results

Many hours spent inspecting a construction site and poring over plans resulted in this pencil sketch of a subsurface chunk of New York.

aren't as natural," explained the artist. "There's a tendency to get more interested in the mechanics than the aesthetics. Believe me, you'll spend all the time you want with the mechanics later!"

With the sketch approved, Foley began building the intersection on his Macintosh computer using a 3-D modeling program called InifiniD. His initial challenge was to prepare the cutaway model so that all the important underground features presented themselves from one point of view.

The model started out as a complex skeletal structure called a wireframe. The artist built the model in sections so he could manipulate different features to get the best view of them. "I recall spending a lot of time pulling sewers out and pushing subway platforms back," says Foley.

Satisfied with the model, Foley converted his snapshots from New York into "texture maps" and applied them to various surfaces of the wireframe. Another feature called a "bump map" controls the smoothness of the textured surface. With the right bumps, textures, and lighting, the model began to assume a realistic appearance. Foley sent several sketches—this time computer generated—that explored the model from different vantage points.

Being able to show several different, but accurate, perspective views is a specific advantage that computer graphic artists have over those who use traditional techniques. The traditional method for developing a sketch of this sort involves a carefully constructed perspective drawing of an object. Once an artist chooses a point of view using the perspective method, he or she is locked into it and must start from scratch for any other vantage point. An artist building a computer model can choose to see the object from an infinite number of viewpoints with little effort. This is a distinct advantage for artist and art director alike, providing each with great flexibility.

Foley's computer model was a great representation of what the new subway station at the intersection of 42nd and Broadway would look like. It was dramatic and accurate, but I felt that we needed to provide more information about what was under New York's streets. There were steam pipes, old sewer tunnels, and different subway lines close to that subway station, but not close enough to make it into the artist's cutaway scene. We had missed something by attempting to stick closely to the information we had obtained from the engineers. We decided to change our plans and create a generic scene based on the subway

Comments from construction site engineers dot an early digital sketch (right). Artist Don Foley constructed a wireframe model (below) consisting of hundreds of individual elements. Assigning different colors to objects helped him keep track of their placement in the scene.

station, but including other underground features commonly found under New York. This immediately freed Foley to add a silver subway train, an old brick sewer, and a parking garage, among other things.

The last step for a computer model is called rendering. With the push of a button, you tell the computer that you want it to output an image of the model in very fine detail. This is what a publisher needs in order to print the image. Foley's model had a whopping 56 different textures applied to hundreds of objects. A model of that complexity sucks computer brain power like soda through a straw. The artist's computer needed five days of uninterrupted thinking to render a final version of the art. Still the art was not complete.

Foley wanted to add people to the diagram to give it life. He spent a Sunday afternoon on top of a parking garage at a shopping mall photographing people from three different angles so as to place them in correct perspective in his model.

Foley then "blurred" his people photos in a digital manipulation program called Adobe Photoshop and merged them with the image of the model. Many people mistake the result for a photograph. "My goal is to not have it look like my image was done on a computer," says the artist.

Foley's art, as well as that of other computer artists who work for NATIONAL GEOGRAPHIC, approaches photo-realism. This is possible only when artists pay close attention to every detail. Anything particularly unrealistic can ruin the effect of the whole scene. The artist's attention to seemingly insignificant details, such as the subway signs and the newspaper dispenser in Foley's final diagram (opposite), contributes to the overall effect.

The "Under New York" diagram took two months to complete. It is not unusual for a computer graphics project to take even longer. This shatters the commonly held misconception that computer art is quicker than traditional methods. The long rendering time for complex models like Foley's is actually a liability as a deadline approaches. It makes last minute changes difficult and time consuming at a stage when things need to happen quickly.

Foley's "Under New York" cutaway diagram earned him more jobs from NATIONAL GEOGRAPHIC. Each new assignment has involved peering under the surface of something, be it the hull of the U.S.S. *Maine* or the Hubble Space Telescope. "I want it to seem like I have a huge X-ray vision machine," says Foley. Sometimes we think he does.
                                                                    —*Chris Sloan*

Abandoned utility pipes

Gas vault

Telecommunications and electrical cables

Electrical vault

Steam pipe

Water main

Gas pipe

Sewer pipe

orm ain

Token booth

Turnstiles

Parking garage

Foundation

Cap

Pile

Electrified third rail

Ventilation duct

Newsstand

Crossover platform

Telecommunications and electrical cables

Subway drainpipe

Sewer main

How Things Work

Leonardo da Vinci believed that to depict the physical world accurately one must understand its underlying processes. He observed the movement of water and the growth of plants and filled his notebooks with explorations of the mechanics of human biology, astronomy, and machines.

Half a millennium later, NATIONAL GEOGRAPHIC artists have revisited some of his favorite themes. Here you will find an explanation of human vision by Ed Gazsi. Greg Harlin illustrates the formation of shadowy umbras and penumbras during an eclipse. Earth science, human reproduction, and hydrodynamics appear as well. Even David Kimble's detailed cutaway of Ford's Model T assembly line and Bruce Morser's anatomy of a factory trawler echo Leonardo's fascination with things mechanical.

Art and science formed an enduring relationship during the Renaissance, driven by the need to understand new concepts and enlighten the public. That need has grown exponentially as scientific education has gained importance in our society. Much has changed in the last 500 years, but thankfully, we still have artists who, like Leonardo, search beyond first impressions for the hidden truths that make our world tick.

CENTER OF THE EARTH

Illustration by CHUCK CARTER *and* ALLEN CARROLL

Imagine a NATIONAL GEOGRAPHIC story published with just two small photographs. This gatefold diagram begins a 12-page story on scientific theories of the center of the earth—old and new. Nine diagrams and one map take over where photographs could not go.

Authors of the 1996 article, Keay Davidson and A. R. Williams, tell of complex research issues in studying the center of the earth: Lacking a means for exploring deeper than 7.5 miles (a borehole in Kola Peninsula in Russia), scientists are only beginning to come close to an understanding of plate tectonics and a more accurate model of the earth, "Researchers working in the fields of seismology, geodynamics, geochemistry and mineral physics ponder where this planet has been and what will become of it.

"Some 4.6 billion years ago, a cloud of dust condensed into planet Earth, which soon turned molten from meteorite impacts and radioactive decay. As it cooled, heavier materials sank, forming a layered globe 8,000 miles in diameter. Still cooling, the earth roils from its core, bringing heat to the surface for release. This convection creates earthquakes and volcanoes that shape our life-bearing lands and seas."

Illustrator Chuck Carter and art director Allen Carroll teamed up to explain, visually, new developments in the search for what lies beneath Earth's surface.

NATIONAL GEOGRAPHIC—January 1996

CONTINENTS
Colliding continental plates form a mountain range. Land may be insulating, trapping heat in the underlying part of the mantle and leading to eventual rifting and breakup.

SUBDUCTION
When two plates collide, one dives beneath the other, eventually becoming part of the earth's mantle. It melts, releasing lava that erupts through the overriding plate as volcanoes. Subduction often causes massive earthquakes.

SEAFLOOR SPREADING
Adjacent plates below the oceans separate at mid-ocean ridges. Magma fills the gap, hardens and attaches to the shifting plates. More magma moves up.

HOT SPOTS
Rising from deep in the mantle, a plume of hot rock melts into the crust and forms a volcano. As the crust moves above the mantle, the plume creates a volcanic chain, leaving old, cold cones at one end and fueling a new active one at the other. This occurs in places such as the Hawaiian Islands.

MAGNETIC FIELD
Earth's magnetic field can point north or south. Over the eons it has reversed itself many times.

RESTLESS MANTLE
Warm rock rises to displace cooler rock, which then sinks, warms up, and rises again to release some 80 percent of the internal heat that the earth radiates.

THE OUTER CORE
Many forces affect this liquid metallic layer. Earth's rotation and convection combine to create columns of spiraling liquid parallel to the earth's rotational axis. As in an electromagnet, the mechanical energy of the spirals generates electricity, which then creates the earth's magnetic field.

INNER CORE
Buried by the outer layers, this innermost region is especially hard to read. It probably contains hexagonal iron crystals aligned with the earth's rotational axis and is growing as the outer core solidifies at the boundary. It may anchor the magnetic field, countering the turbulent currents of the outer core.

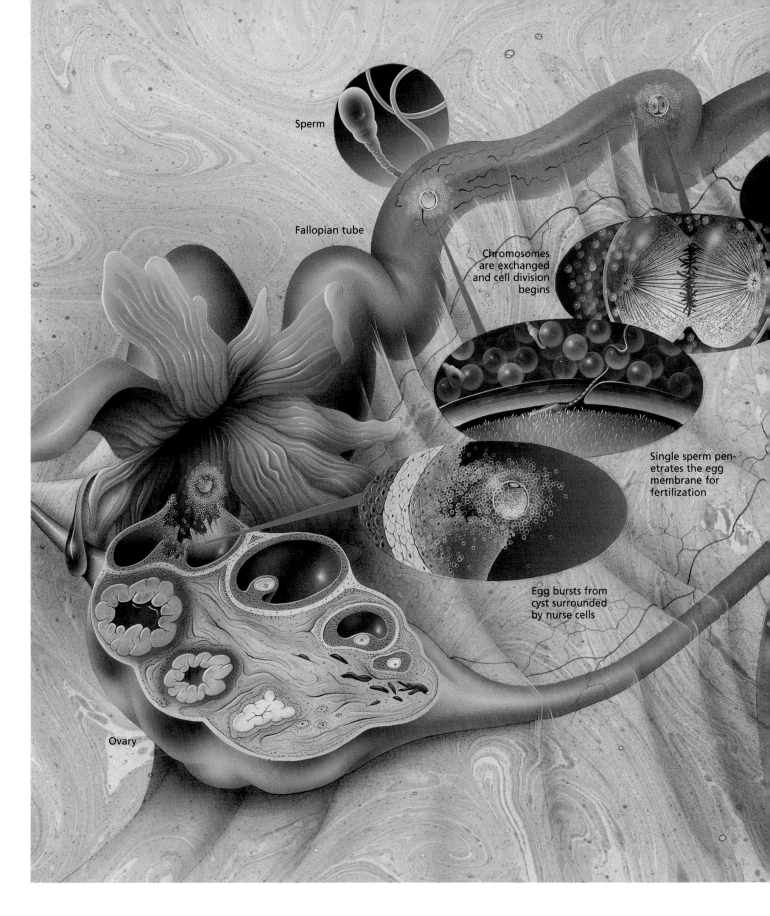

Sperm

Fallopian tube

Chromosomes
are exchanged
and cell division
begins

Single sperm pen-
etrates the egg
membrane for
fertilization

Egg bursts from
cyst surrounded
by nurse cells

Ovary

LIFE BEFORE BIRTH
Illustration by KEITH KASNOT

Looking like the bubbled arrival of the Good Witch of the North in the land of Oz, a fetus at three months has succeeded through a lot of "ifs." For six more months, it can follow a steady yellow brick road of growth before birth.

Beginning at left, an egg is released from an adult human female's ovary every month. Entering into the fallopian tube, it has a chance of being penetrated by a male's sperm. If fertilized, the egg prepares for entering the uterus and for attachment to the wall. If successfully

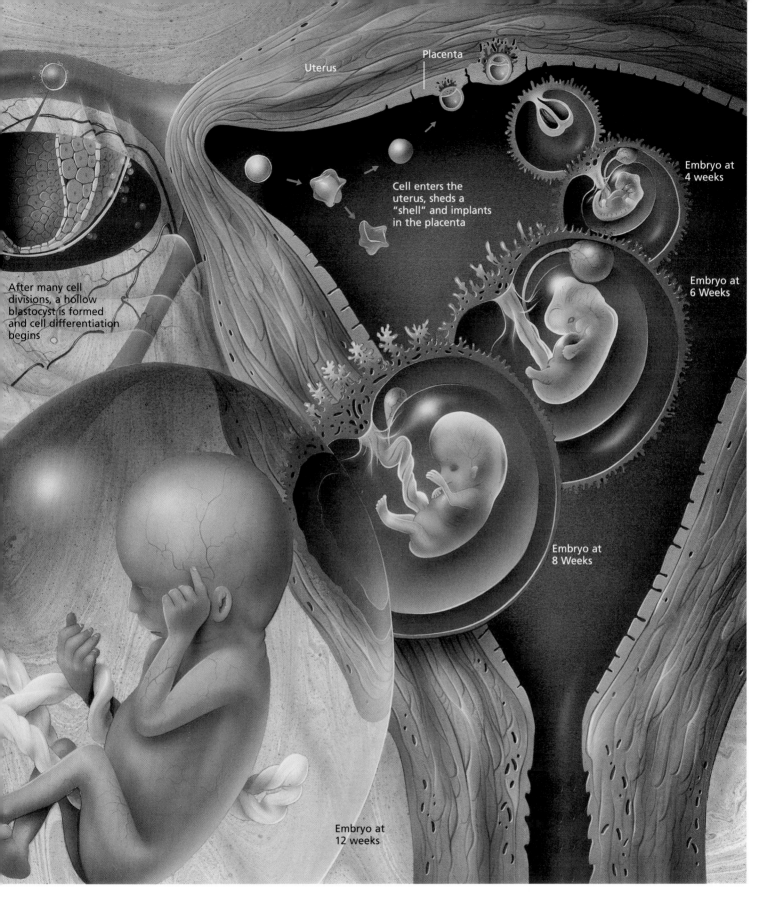

Uterus

Placenta

Cell enters the
uterus, sheds a
"shell" and implants
in the placenta

After many cell
divisions, a hollow
blastocyst is formed
and cell differentiation
begins

Embryo at
4 weeks

Embryo at
6 Weeks

Embryo at
8 Weeks

Embryo at
12 weeks

attached, the embryo develops within a protective and nutritious environment for six more months of steady growth.

This crucial first trimester is beautifully articulated by certified medical illustrator Keith Kasnot. Working in acrylic paint, Kasnot achieved a womb-like background texture by using marbleized paper.

Kasnot worked with an infertility clinic in Arizona, where he lives, and was guided by a medical expert in California. Art director Chris Sloan and researcher Karen Gibbs worked with a clinic in Virginia.

Other research topics for this story led to two more diagrams that covered prenatal screening and in vitro fertilization techniques.

For various reasons, some of the many story ideas generated for the magazine, such as this one, are not published.

Unpublished—1992

Engine block
assembly line

Car bodies placed
on assembly line

Engines mounted
by chain hoist

Gas tank installed
and gas added

Upholstery, top,
and sides attache

FORD PLANT
Illustration by DAVID KIMBLE

"Factories changed forever on April 1, 1913, when 29 Model T Ford workers first stood along an improvised assembly line to produce flywheel magnetos. Rather than assemble an entire magneto himself, each man now performed a single task and moved the unit to the next man. Assembly time immediately fell from 20 minutes per magneto to 13 minutes and, within a year, to 5 after engineers added a chain drive to the line and tinkered to find its optimum speed," reads the published text for this artwork.

The caption for the diagram states: "The 60-acre Highland Park, Michigan, plant, designed by Albert Kahn for easy transit of raw materials and parts through a complex that employed 13,000 workers in 1914 (for clarity far fewer are depicted). Ford's array of 15,000 machines for metal forging, stamping, machining, painting, and baking produced parts—5,000 per car—so similar and reliable that few required hand finishing. Cars were simply started and driven off the line."

Celebrating the 100th anniversary of the Society in 1988, the *Historical Atlas of the United States* was conceived as a gift to the nation, with this diagram illustrating a chapter on industry. The atlas was given free to the 35,000 U.S. public, private, and parochial schools with grades nine or higher. Then President Gilbert M. Grosvenor envisioned it as a "marriage of history to geography that promises to open fertile new ground to both fields."

Historical Atlas of the United States—1988

Mufflers and
exhaust pipes
attached

Five-ton capacity
electric crane

ngine block
nilling

Punch presses

Tires mounted
on wheels

Wheels and
radiators
attached

Radiators filled,
cars started and
driven offline

LUNAR ECLIPSE
The moon passes into earth's umbral shadow, an event visible to half the planet at once. Bathed in light refracted by earth's atmosphere, the moon appears reddish.

Penumbra   Umbra

PARTIAL SOLAR ECLIPSE
From earth's perspective, the moon does not cover the entire sun, only the penumbra touches earth.

ANNULAR SOLAR ECLIPSE
For more than half its orbit the moon's apparent size is smaller than the sun's, allowing a ring of the photosphere to surround the moon.

TOTAL SOLAR ECLIPSE
As the moon completely blocks the sun, the corona is visible above the solar surface.

THE GALLERY OF ECLIPSES
Illustration by GREG HARLIN

Casting a shadow on earth not only sheds light on understanding eclipses but also provides information about the source of the light—the sun.

"A Gallery of Eclipses" defines (top to bottom) lunar, partial solar, annular solar, and total solar eclipses. The published text explains the glorious conjunction: "In a coincidence unmatched in the solar system, the sun's diameter is 400 times that of the moon, and the moon is about 400 times closer to the earth than the sun. That combination allows the moon to cover the sun's disk as it passes between the earth and sun. Were the moon's diameter 140 miles less, totality (when the lunar and solar rims fit like stacked spoons) would not occur; viewers would never see the corona.

"Historians have dated events from long ago by using accounts of eclipses. A Chinese scribe may have been the first to document one 4,000 years ago.

"Total solar eclipses are doomed to extinction. If the moon continues to recede from the earth at about an inch a year—in a billion years it will be too far away to cover the sun."

"It's all about the idea of light," explains art director Nick Kirilloff. Light is visible when it is reflected off objects. In space there is nothing for the light to reflect off. In order to help the reader "see" the eclipses, the texture of this background was created by imagining that the light is hitting a "room filled with dust" rather than the vast emptiness of space.

Kirilloff enjoys working with Greg Harlin, who stretched beyond his usual technique to find a way to make this conception happen. "We spoke the same language of design," he says.

NATIONAL GEOGRAPHIC—May 1992

Skidi Pawnee

Egyptian

Moche and Chimu

Greek

ORION
Illustration by JOE TUCCIARONE

Igniting imagination, religion, and scientific query, stars of the constellation Orion are diagrammed to explain what photographs of the sky cannot. Although they appear equidistant to human eyes, the stars spread 500 and 2,000 light-years from earth.

The dominant constellation in the winter sky, the stars of Orion illustrated stories of various cultures, shaping a hunter to ancient Greeks, while the ancient Egyptians saw their crowned god Osiris riding in his boat. To the Moche and Chimu of South America, the stars illustrate punishment of a thief whose heart is eaten by buzzards. Skidi Pawnee saw three deer rising in the sky.

This diagram, with its connect-the-dots look at the stars, enables us to visualize these stories from our modern and more literal point of view.

Contracted for his expertise in painting astronomy subjects and for his perspective drawing skills, Joe Tucciarone supplemented the same Orion article with other diagrams depicting the birth of stars and the intricate nebulae.

NATIONAL GEOGRAPHIC—December 1995

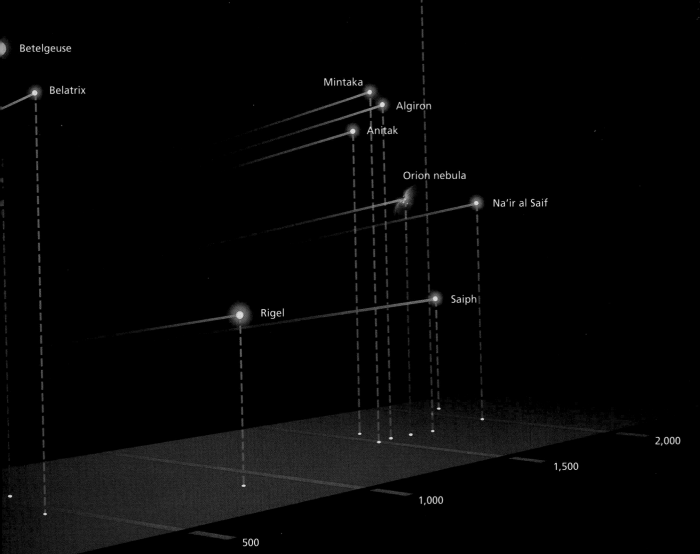

Meissa

Betelgeuse

Belatrix

Mintaka

Algiron

Anitak

Orion nebula

Na'ir al Saif

Saiph

Rigel

2,000

1,500

1,000

500

Distances from earth in light-years

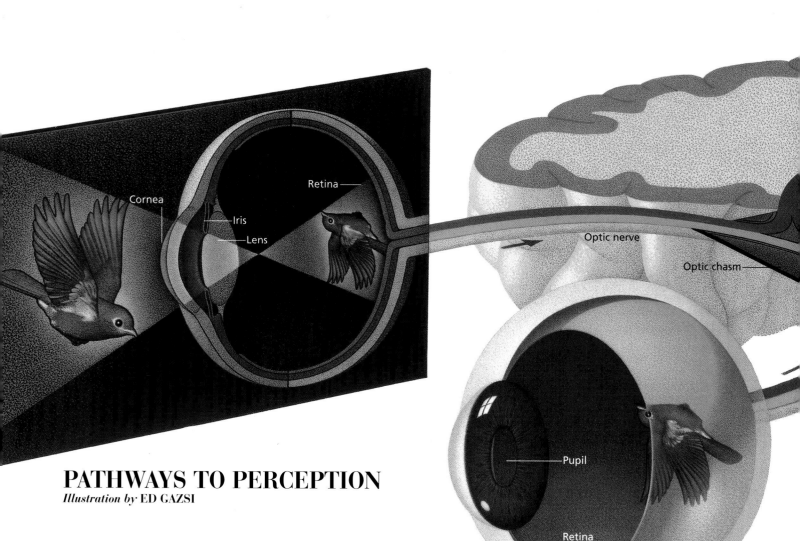

PATHWAYS TO PERCEPTION
Illustration by ED GAZSI

Using half a brain for this diagram made the process of human eyesight easier to understand. It was important for getting the perfect cross section in which the pathways of perception are visible.

Here, artist Ed Gazsi shows, in a schematic diagram, essential elements for healthy sight: 1) the eye as a camera, 2) the retina, 3) left and right channels of optic nerves, 4) the switchboard—receiving and transmitting neural information, 5) putting all the pieces of information together, and 6) recognition and positioning.

The published text explains: "The act of seeing a bird on the wing (above) begins as our camera-like lenses focus the image, upside down, on the retina at the back of each eye. Within this sliver of neural tissue, millions of photo-receptor cells parse the image into an array of components. The bird's color, shape, and motion—each flick of feather and glint of eye—are received as photons of light and coded into tiny electrical impulses.

"In a feat of computation that far exceeds that of any computer, the impulses are channeled to the cortex, where they are analyzed and interpreted. Finally, the brain creates our perception of the bird, instantly and right side up, in a manner that scientists can only partly explain."

To obtain the appropriate visual reference material, researcher Hillel Hoffmann ordered a human brain from a biological supply company and found an expert to make the slice. Not the usual office supply order, the invoice "Human Brain $400" is still the talk of the Purchasing Division.

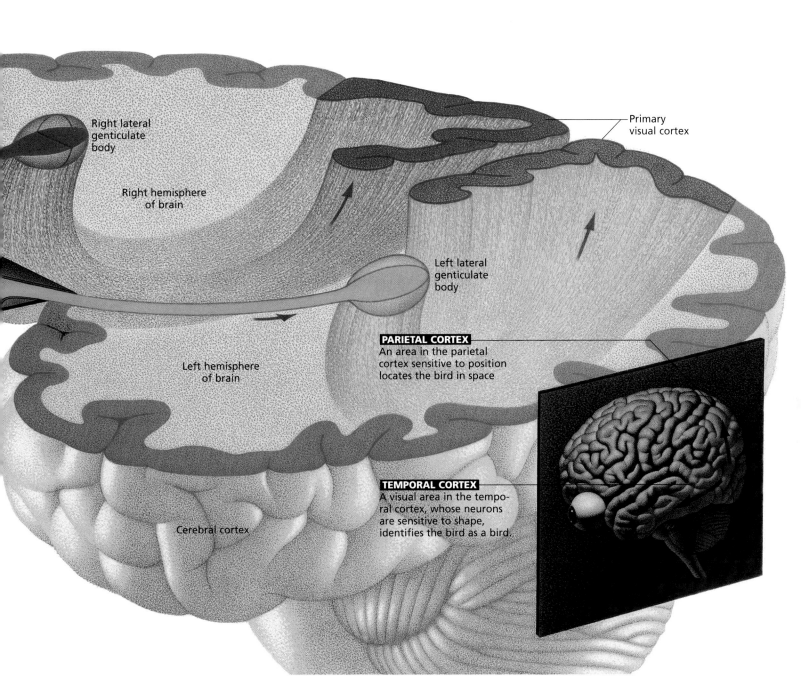

Right lateral
genticulate
body

Right hemisphere
of brain

Left lateral
genticulate
body

Primary
visual cortex

Left hemisphere
of brain

PARIETAL CORTEX
An area in the parietal
cortex sensitive to position
locates the bird in space

TEMPORAL CORTEX
A visual area in the temporal cortex, whose neurons
are sensitive to shape,
identifies the bird as a bird.

Cerebral cortex

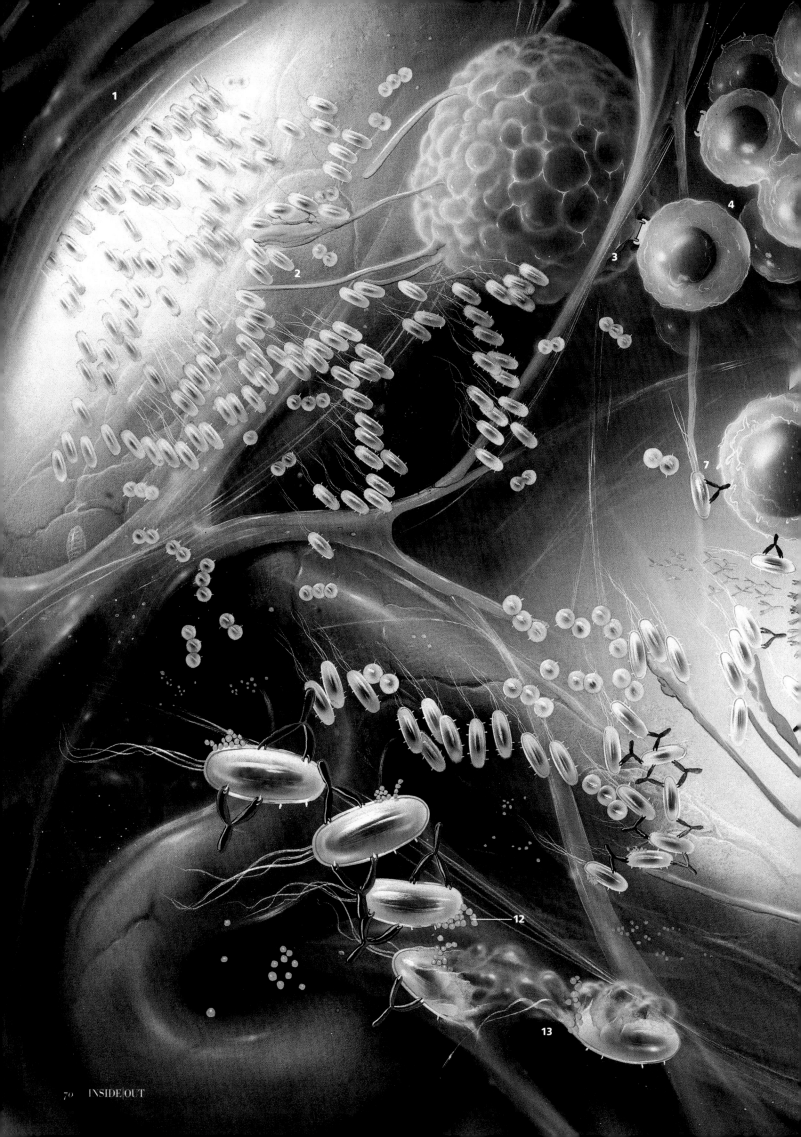

BACTERIAL INVASION
Illustration by CARL ROHRIG

Within a lymph node, the text published with the art reads, "A battle rages between the body's attackers and defenders. Bacteria pour in through a lymphatic channel (1). A macrophage engulfs the invaders (2), digests them, and displays their identity markers on its own surface. The macrophage presents this chemical message to a white blood cell known as a helper T-cell (3). The T-cell responds to the urgent message by multiplying (4). Its progeny release lymphokines, chemical messages that call more defenders to arms (5). Some T-cells send a signal to new fighters—known as B-cells—telling them to join the battle (6). Only B-cells specially programmed to recognize this specific kind of bacterium are put on alert. The B-cells link up with the bacteria and begin to reproduce (7). Some new B-cells become memory cells that store information to help the body fight the same kind of bacterium on another day (8). Other B-cells become plasma cells and join the battle, spewing out thousands of antibodies each second (9). Like guided missiles, the antibodies home in on the bacteria, forcing them to clump together (10). Macrophages sweep through, swallowing the clumped bacteria (11). A group of protein molecules—called complement—helps antibodies make bacteria into palatable morsels for macrophages (12). Or complement may kill bacteria directly by puncturing their cell walls (13). Scavenging macrophages will clean the lymph node of battle debris, engulfing scattered antibodies, complement, and dead bacteria until the infection finally subsides."

Illustrator Carl Rohrig's advertisement in an artists' annual catalogue caught the attention of art director David Seager. *The Incredible Machine* included a number of Rohrig's diagrams of human body functions.

The Incredible Machine—1986

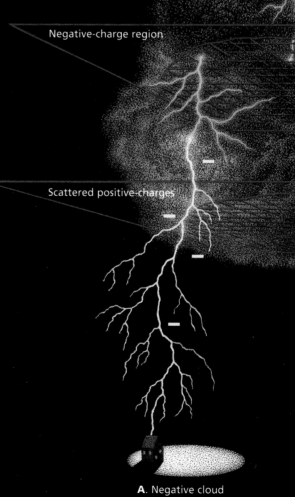

Positive-charge region

E. Intraclou

Negative-charge region

Scattered positive-charges

LIGHTNING
Illustration by EDWARD S. GAZSI

When thunder rumbles from the heavens, angels may very well be bowling as some children believe. But consultant Martin Uman from the University of Florida guided researcher David Wooddell, art director Mark Holmes, and artist Ed Gazsi through the grown-up theory of how lightning strikes and produces thunder.

Text published with the art explains: "A cloud-to-ground lightning flash throbs with more electricity than could be produced by all U.S. generators combined during that instant. Yet the flash is so brief that the electric energy where it strikes would power a light bulb for only a month or so. Virtually all lightning energy is converted into light, thunder, radio waves, and heat. The peak temperature of 55,000° F in the channel lasts a few millionths of a second—barely long enough to singe a victim's clothes.

"As a thundercloud billows, rising ice crystals collide with falling hailstones. The hail strips electrons from the ice. The top of the cloud becomes predominantly positive and the bottom mostly negative, with scattered positive areas at its base (large diagram at right). Negative charges in the lower cloud induce a positive region, or 'shadow,' on the earth below. Static electricity builds, and a negative spark is launched from the lower cloud by a yet unknown trigger.

"The descending spark creates jagged, branched channels; upward sparks sprout like weeds from the ground. When an upward and a downward spark meet, the stroke we see spreads in both directions, superheating air and creating shock waves that produce thunder.

"Both negative cloud-to-ground lightning (A) and positive ground-to-cloud lightning (C) connect negative cloud regions with the ground. Other types (B, D) link the top of the cloud and the ground. Lightning in and among clouds (E, F), a hazard to planes, is often seen from earth as sheets of light."

This diagram serves as a glossary of lightning terms, rounding out a story of astounding photographs—lightning in nature and lab—affecting skyscrapers and airplanes, football players and swimmers.

NATIONAL GEOGRAPHIC—July 1993

A. Negative cloud to ground

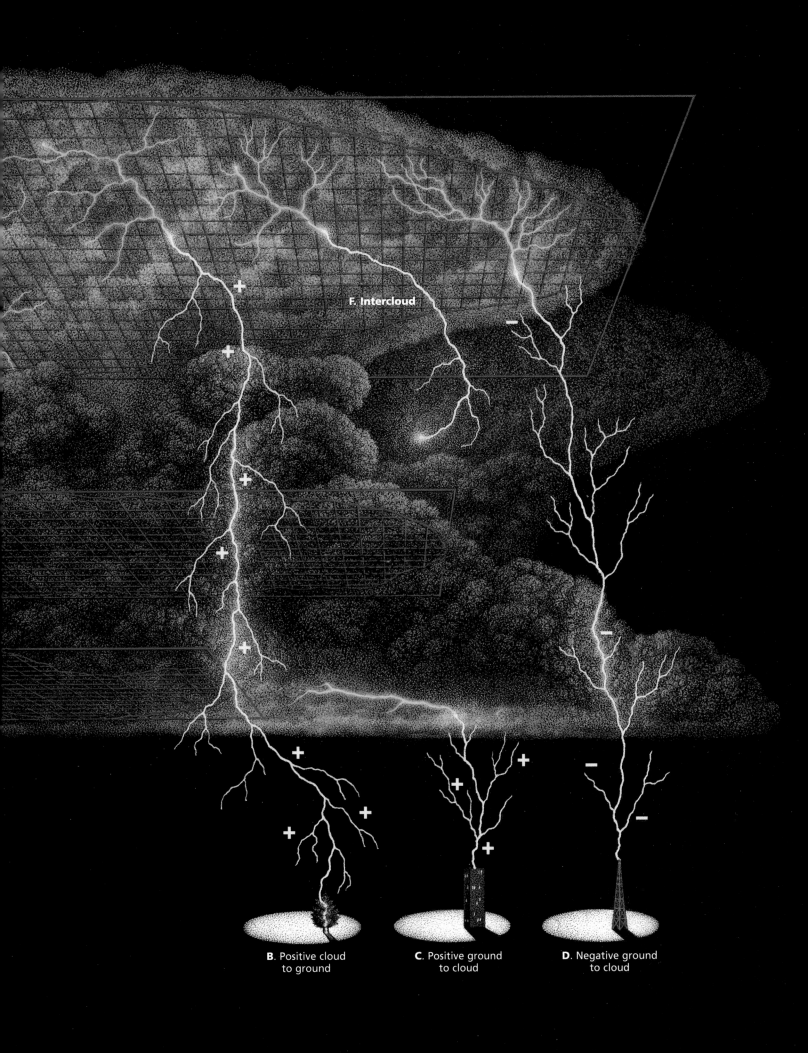

F. Intercloud

B. Positive cloud
to ground

C. Positive ground
to cloud

D. Negative ground
to cloud

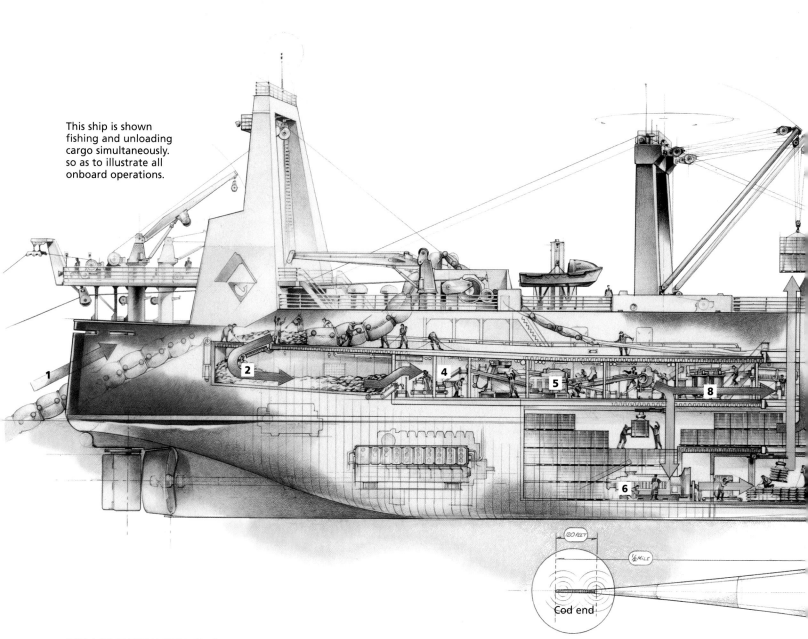

This ship is shown fishing and unloading cargo simultaneously. so as to illustrate all onboard operations.

Cod end

Sensors on the "cod end," or tip, of the net alert the crew to the volume of fish caught in each trawl.

HARVESTERS OF THE HIGH SEAS
Illustration by BRUCE MORSER

"More than a million fishing vessels now sift the world's oceans for seafood—twice as many as in 1970. Yet the global fleet, subsidized for decades by national governments, is poised for a major downsizing," reads the original text. "'Many of the small mom-and-pop operations are going to be left behind,' says an expert with the U.S. National Marine Fisheries Service. 'The trend is going toward fewer, bigger, more efficient boats.' The *Alaska Ocean* (above) could be a flagship for this new era of industrial fishing. Based in Anacortes, Washington, the ship can process more than 600 metric tons of pollock a day into *surimi*, the protein paste used in imitation seafood products. At 376 feet she is one of the largest factory trawlers in the world. Once brought aboard (1), the catch is spilled into a fish bin (2) while the half-mile-long net is spooled onto a reel (3). The fish are weighed (4) and then gutted and cleaned (5). Nothing is wasted; offal is processed into fish meal (6) and stored (7). Fish fillets are washed, bleached, and treated with additives (8) before being squeezed into surimi paste (9). Blocks of surimi are then quick-frozen (10) before being boxed and stored in the refrigerated hold (11). To boost morale among 125 crew members, living decks (12) are separated from work decks. Amenities include a brass-trimmed cafeteria, a gymnasium, bathrooms with Japanese soaking tubs, and televisions in most cabins."

Good friendships are sometimes made over good diagrams. Artist Bruce Morser and world-renowned ship architect Guido Perla were teamed up after researcher Hillel Hoffmann and art director Chris Sloan discovered that the two live on the same island. Over six months and a dozen sketches, Perla and Morser found their common interest while touring the fishing vessel and consulting on sketches. Morser had an enormous amount of information from which to work. An artist's first-hand knowledge of a subject usually shows in the details, as the inner workings of the *Alaska Ocean* attest.

NATIONAL GEOGRAPHIC—November 1995

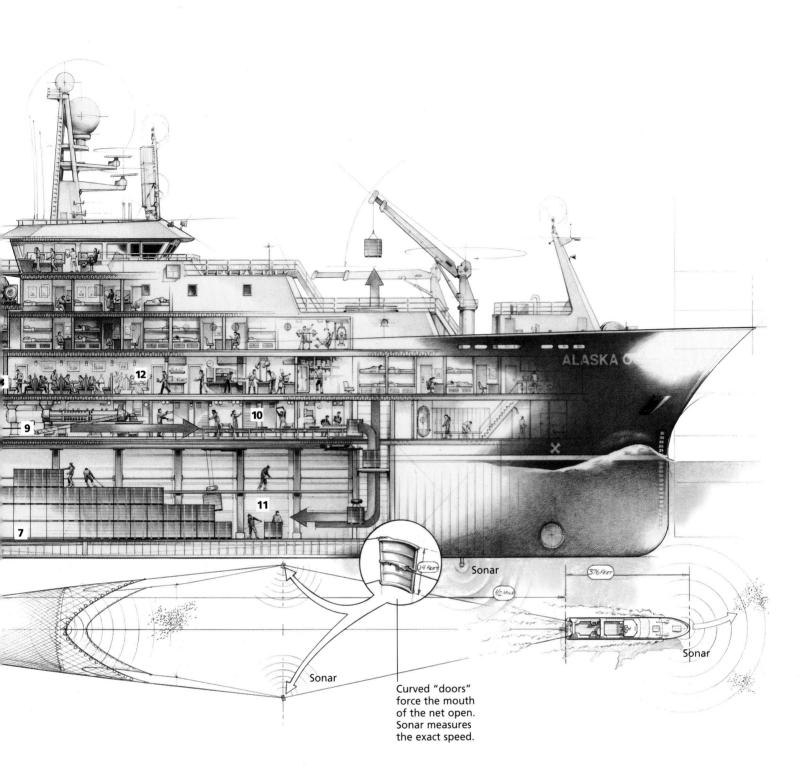

Curved "doors"
force the mouth
of the net open.
Sonar measures
the exact speed.

Sonar

Sonar

Sonar

ALASKA O

12

9

10

11

7

Aperture door

Light enters
front aperture

High-gain
antenna

Secondary
mirror

Primary
mirror

Fine
guidance
sensor

STIS
(Space Telescope
Imaging System)

Solar
array

NICMOS
(Near-Infrared
Camera and
Multi-Object
Spectrometer)

AN EYE IN SPACE
Illustration by DON FOLEY

"In 1923 German scientist Hermann Oberth proposed an orbiting telescope above earth's distorting atmosphere," published text explains. "Hubble was launched in 1990—four months after Oberth's death. Rebounding from early problems, Hubble is unrivaled for its clarity of view.

"In 1997, several new devices were scheduled for installation. An imaging spectrograph (STIS) gives vital information about galaxy composition and dynamics; a near-infrared camera (NICMOS) enables Hubble to see inside dust clouds.

"In 1999, the advanced Camera for Surveys will increase Hubble's light sensitivity by a factor of ten. NASA also plans to replace Hubble's solar panels with smaller, more efficient units.

"In 2002, on the final servicing mission, instruments will be added that may enable Hubble to function past its planned 15-year life span."

Artist Don Foley, whose expertise in computer-generated illustration has resulted in two books on digital art, is a fast and efficient illustrator. Art director Nick Kirilloff was amazed to see his studio, where Foley works on several computer monitors at the same time for different parts or angles of the same illustration.

NATIONAL GEOGRAPHIC—April 1997

ISLAND FORMATION
Illustration by BRUCE MORSER

I t may be a little like asking a young child to sit perfectly still for longer than an hour—it's not natural. Children have to move or they fidget and squirm.

Shifting sands and time continually alter the barrier islands of the Atlantic and Gulf coasts of the United States. Nature created hundreds of islands that buffer the mainland from storms, but modern humans' love of beaches—in the form of development—is holding back the islands' natural inclination to move.

In this four-part diagram, artist Bruce Morser uses Assateague as an example, as the accompanying text explains: "(1) The island, rimmed by a sound and tidal inlets, builds itself as incoming waves dredge up bottom sediment and deposit it onshore, where winds sweep it into dunes. Sheltered by the dunes, a marsh

develops on the sound side of the island, and plants and forests take root. When storm waves inevitably break through the dunes (2), sand invades the backcountry, covering vegetation, while surf levels the dunes (3). As sands wash over Assateague, it migrates landward (4), leaving remnants of salt marsh peat behind on the new beach."

Diagrams illustrating sequential steps, like this one, have been published in the magazine for many years. Like time-lapse photography, they show movement on a printed page. Often sequence diagrams accompany maps, and employ deep colors and a precise style. Here, art-directed by Jeff Osborn, Morser uses soft colors and a technique reminiscent of mechanical drawings to loosen the style.

NATIONAL GEOGRAPHIC—August 1997

GLACIER FORMATION
Illustration by
LLOYD K. TOWNSEND

W hat beautiful NATIONAL GEOGRAPHIC photographs of the Arctic cannot describe is that a glacier moves—surges, actually—and it groans. While a diagram can't groan either, it can show the dynamics of how a glacier moves.

The text block accompanying the art states: "A glacier is a slow-motion river of ice. It flows from high mountain peaks through rocky valleys, carrying off unmelted snow that has compacted over many years into a solid, creeping ice stream.

"The ice flows like a conveyor belt, driven by gravity and the ever mounting snows behind it in an area called the accumulation zone. In the lower region, or ablation zone, the glacier loses ice through melting and evaporation. If they are in balance, with enough new ice added to replace the loss, the glacier is stable, with little advance or retreat. If the balance is tipped, it shifts accordingly.

"In Alaska, only a few glaciers reach the sea, pushing out across the floor of a bay, fjord, or seacoast. The advancing ice scrapes and grinds the bedrock, boulders, and gravel beneath it and pushes ahead of itself a ridge or terminal moraine of rock and earth. It helps to anchor the glacier's face. There, the ice breaks off as icebergs— a process called calving—balancing the flow of ice from behind."

NATIONAL GEOGRAPHIC—January 1987

Accumulation zone

Ablation zone

Terminal moraine

Calving

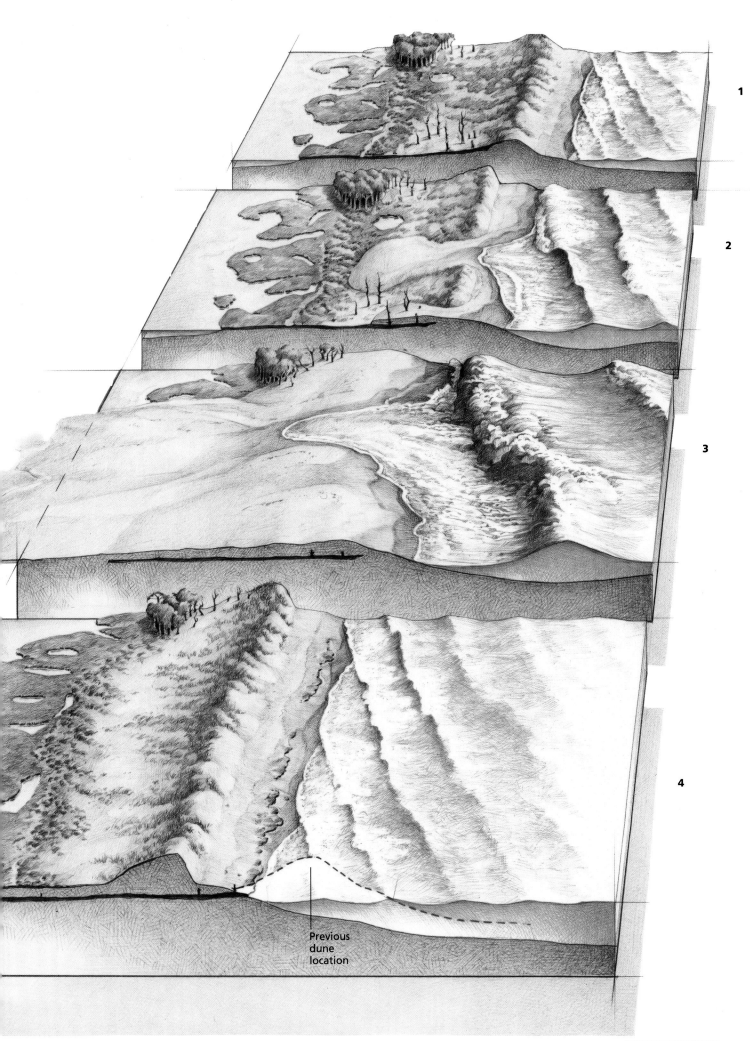

1

2

3

Previous
dune
location

4

130 mph winds

3. Vortex spin hits 80 mph. Traveling at 120 mph, the 80 mph winds have a 200 mph punch, ruining homes in mere seconds.

2. Vortex stretches and increases to 40 mph, causing winds of 160 mph.

ANDREW'S RECKLESS RIDE
Illustration by DAVIS MELTZER

Creating a publishing deadline nearly as whirlwind as the subject it depicts, "Andrew's Reckless Ride" was completed in three months to provide a timely report on the third strongest hurricane to touch the U.S. mainland this century. Photography and text reported on the devastation to human and animal lives, property, and the environment. By diagramming the science of hurricane research, the artwork explained how the damage occurred in America's Sunshine State.

Consultant Ted Fujita, professor emeritus of the University of Chicago, whose theory of spin-up vortices (top) is depicted for the first time in a popular magazine, led the explanation of hurricane dynamics. According to the published text, "Currents of warm, moist air (purple arrows, center) spiral toward the voracious low-pressure eye. As the air rises, water vapor condenses, releasing heat that fuels hurricane winds. In Andrew, some updrafts raged with rare intensity, spawning destructive vortices beneath them."

Cartography was added to the diagram (lower left) to track the four days Hurricane Andrew ravaged the Bahamas, South Florida, and Louisiana. "Damage could have been worse, however. Andrew's destructive path across the far south of Florida raced at nearly 20 miles an hour, twice the usual pace for hurricanes in this region. Had the eye struck Miami and Fort Lauderdale, scores more might have died. Had it lingered, more wildlife might have perished," as the text explained.

Artist Davis Meltzer, whose legendary use of bold acrylic color belies a gentle nature, captured the mechanics of the hurricane. The assignment disturbed him, though—Hurricane Andrew brought on so much damage, so much heartache.

NATIONAL GEOGRAPHIC—April 1993

Intense
updraft

1. Vortex spinning
at 20 mph and
traveling with
winds averaging
120 mph combine
to create winds
of 140 mph.

110 mph winds

Intense
updraft

Center of eye

DADE COUNTY

Fort
Lauderdale

THE EVERGLADES

Miami

Homestead
Florida City

Path of eye

Everglades National Park

Finding the Secret to the Beluga's Song

Observing beluga whales was an important part of the assignment for artist Keith Kasnot. His photos, below, helped as reference in creating the diagram.

In 1993 NATIONAL GEOGRAPHIC planned a story on beluga whales, the beautiful white animals that look like floating bars of ivory soap when they congregate in the ice floes of northern waters. Nicknamed "sea canaries" by sailors, these animals are the kings of cacophony compared to other cetaceans. How do they produce these sounds? Art researcher Hillel Hoffmann and I decided that illustrating the beluga's sound-generating mechanism would be a good theme for a diagram. Illustrations editor Bob Patton, in charge of the photography and overall direction of the story, agreed.

Little did we know that finding out how these beasts produced their chorus would require a coast-to-coast cast of experts and the talents of Arizona-based medical illustrator Keith Kasnot. Hoffmann searched for scientists who worked with belugas. Dr. Kenneth Norris, author of the story and a whale expert himself, referred Hoffmann to a researcher at Woods Hole Oceanographic Institution in Massachusetts, who had been taping beluga sounds. He also mentioned that the U.S. Navy was studying belugas at a research facility in San Diego.

Recorded beluga calls may sound great on a tape player, but what good were they to a magazine? Hoffmann contacted Dr. Cheri Recchia at Woods Hole to find out. Recchia told him that to study the whale sounds she converted them into graphic images called sonograms. She had sonograms of clicks, claps, and twitters, as well as high-frequency emanations inaudible to the human ear. These high-frequency clicking sounds are part of the beluga's sophisticated echolocation capability.

That's where the Navy came in. At the Naval Research and Development Laboratory in San Diego, Drs. Sam Ridgeway and Ted Cranford were studying the cranial anatomy of belugas to learn everything possible about their natural sonar. Their research could lead to improvements in man-made sonar used on boats and submarines. When first contacted, the scientists indicated there was still some uncertainty regarding the source of the full range of beluga sounds. Despite this, the scientists were kind enough to invite us out to learn what we could.

Earlier that year, I had worked with artist Keith Kasnot on a project called "Life Before Birth." (see pages 60-61). Kasnot impressed me with his artistic ability as well as his knowledge of anatomy. Now I needed someone to illustrate the

This is an absolute bear to illustrate and I know the beluga is a bit different than dolphins but have dissected only one beluga + can't state accurately.

Rabbit ears

a view of melon alone, without airways to confuse things.

melon

melon branches and ends in rabbit ears one on each side of the airway just below where it dumps into uppermost (vestibular) sac + then the blowhole is above.

Blowhole

vestibular sac

Premaxillary sac (lies right on top of skull).

Bony nares (where paired nasal passages pierce the skull)

melon

skull

I've stippled fat + lined air spaces

In the beluga the soft pliable melon goes right to the surface of the forehead + can be severely deformed.

Teeth are 9-9 in upper jaws and 8-8 in lower and only in front ½ of jaw. note how they splay out.

The outline of the whale's head is quite good. The lips can be pursed in a perfect tube (see Xerox). Its the anatomy of the sac system of the superior nares that are awful and the diagram of sound emission (sound mirrors). I can't tell ... about the whistle, clap, jaw clap, echolocating click, since ... I don't know how you plan to represent them...

The artist's struggle with the complexity of beluga anatomy is illustrated by these sketches, including the comment-peppered fax page from a scientist shown above. At right are "monkey lips"—the suspected locus of many of the noises.

inner workings of a whale's head. Could Kasnot do it? "No problem," he told me. Reflecting back on that moment, the artist says, "I had never been asked to illustrate an animal before. I felt, however, that with my background in anatomy, physiology, and the other 'ologies,' I could illustrate just about any living thing." I asked Kasnot to meet with art researcher Hoffmann and the Navy scientists in San Diego.

For both artist and researcher, the visit to the San Diego naval facility was unforgettable. Dr. Cranford showed them a complex computer model of a beluga head built from cross-sectional CT scans. They also obtained photographs of dissected beluga nasal passages that exposed the suspected sound-generating areas. The locus of the sound seemed to be a small pair of skin flaps affectionately called "monkey lips," which lay in the blowhole passage. Cranford suggested that the lips may vibrate rapidly as air shoots through them, producing sounds that emerge through the jello-like melon, an organ of the whale's forehead.

The highlight of the visit was the docks, where belugas frolicked in large saltwater pools. There they met Muktuk, a trained beluga, who, after initial shyness, became frisky and eager to interact. "I think meeting that whale face-to-face helped Kasnot as much as any of the anatomical information we obtained," says Hoffmann.

"I became enchanted by belugas," says Kasnot. "When I looked Muktuk in the eye, I saw a twinkle—a divine spark."

While Kasnot and Hoffmann concentrated on beluga anatomy, I contacted Dr. Greg Budney at Cornell University's Laboratory of Ornithology. Dr. Budney and his colleagues manage a collection of thousands of taped noises called the Library of Natural Sounds. I asked if it was possible to match Dr. Recchia's beluga sonograms with familiar sounds. Interested in the challenge, Budney spent many hours over the next months comparing the beluga sonograms with those in the library to find good matches. In the end, he found a number of sounds that were excellent matches to the beluga calls. Among them were bird whistles, insect buzzings, and an assortment of other pops, croaks, and trills.

When it came time for Kasnot to begin his artwork, he found that he needed better information on beluga skulls. Hoffmann made probing telephone calls around the country—and even to Russia—asking scientists if they had anything that could help the artist. Nothing turned up. Not easily daunted, Hoffmann recalled seeing a beluga skeleton hanging from a ceiling at Sea World in San Diego. He went into action. "A week or two later a beluga skull arrived on my doorstep via Federal Express," says an amused, but appreciative, Kasnot.

The artist and I worked on several different layout ideas to incorporate the many elements of this project—the whale painting, details of whale anatomy, and the sonograms. The result shows how all the information on an art project comes together onto a magazine page. It also reflects the generous efforts of a variety of people toward helping a NATIONAL GEOGRAPHIC artist show how something works. Thinking back on the project, Kasnot told me, "It was the coolest project I ever worked on." Hoffmann quipped, "Yes, it really clicked."   —*Chris Sloan*

The beluga whale diagram involved many elements that had to work together. Rough layouts, like the one at left, help the artist and art director explore many possibilites before committing to a final design idea (below and following pages).

SON
SEA

Awed by a white-whale symphony, sailors have dubbed belugas sea canaries. Biologists are still trying to learn how—and why—belugas broadcast their vast repertoire of croaks, whistles, and brays.

Many sounds originate from air sacs and organs adjoining the oil-filled melon in a beluga's forehead, as detailed at right. Fatty pouches (dorsal bursae) are embedded in lip-like structures that sputter as air shoots through them. Ted Cranford of the Naval Research and Development Laboratory in San Diego theorizes that the vibrations caused as the bursae slap together are then conducted out through melon oil. Belugas hear through oil lining the lower jaw that sends sound to inner ears.

Below are graphs of common beluga sounds and familiar sounds having similar patterns.

Skull

Melon

Lower jaw

Source of sound
"Lips" in the beluga's air passage help produce staccato sounds. Muscles control the sputter speed.

Muscles that alter melon shape

Beluga buzz saw
Time
Upper limit of human hearing

LOW Frequency HIGH

Meadow grasshopper

Rapid-fire buzzes, pulses, and grunts abound when belugas mill in a group. The cacophony may be a form of social chatter.

Beluga whistle

Songbird

Trills and whistles may help coordinate herd movements. Scientists don't know how belugas make these melodic sounds.

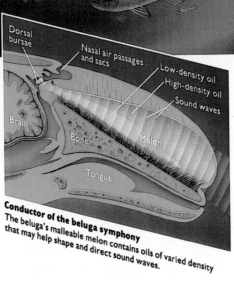

Dorsal bursae

Nasal air passages and sacs

Low-density oil

High-density oil

Sound waves

Brain

Bone

Melon

Tongue

Conductor of the beluga symphony
The beluga's malleable melon contains oils of varied density that may help shape and direct sound waves.

Beluga pop

Hand clap

This explosive bang signals aggression. Other whale species make a similar sound, apparently to startle and debilitate prey.

Beluga echolocation clicks

Upper limit of human hearing

Thousandths of a second apart, high-frequency echolocation clicks act as sonar to help belugas navigate and target prey.

PAINTINGS BY KEITH KASNOT. SPECTROGRAMS AND SOUNDS PROVIDED BY WOODS HOLE OCEANOGRAPHIC INSTITUTION; LIBRARY OF NATURAL SOUND, CORNELL UNIVERSITY LABORATORY OF ORNITHOLOGY; AND CANADIAN DEPARTMENT OF FISHERIES AND OCEANS.

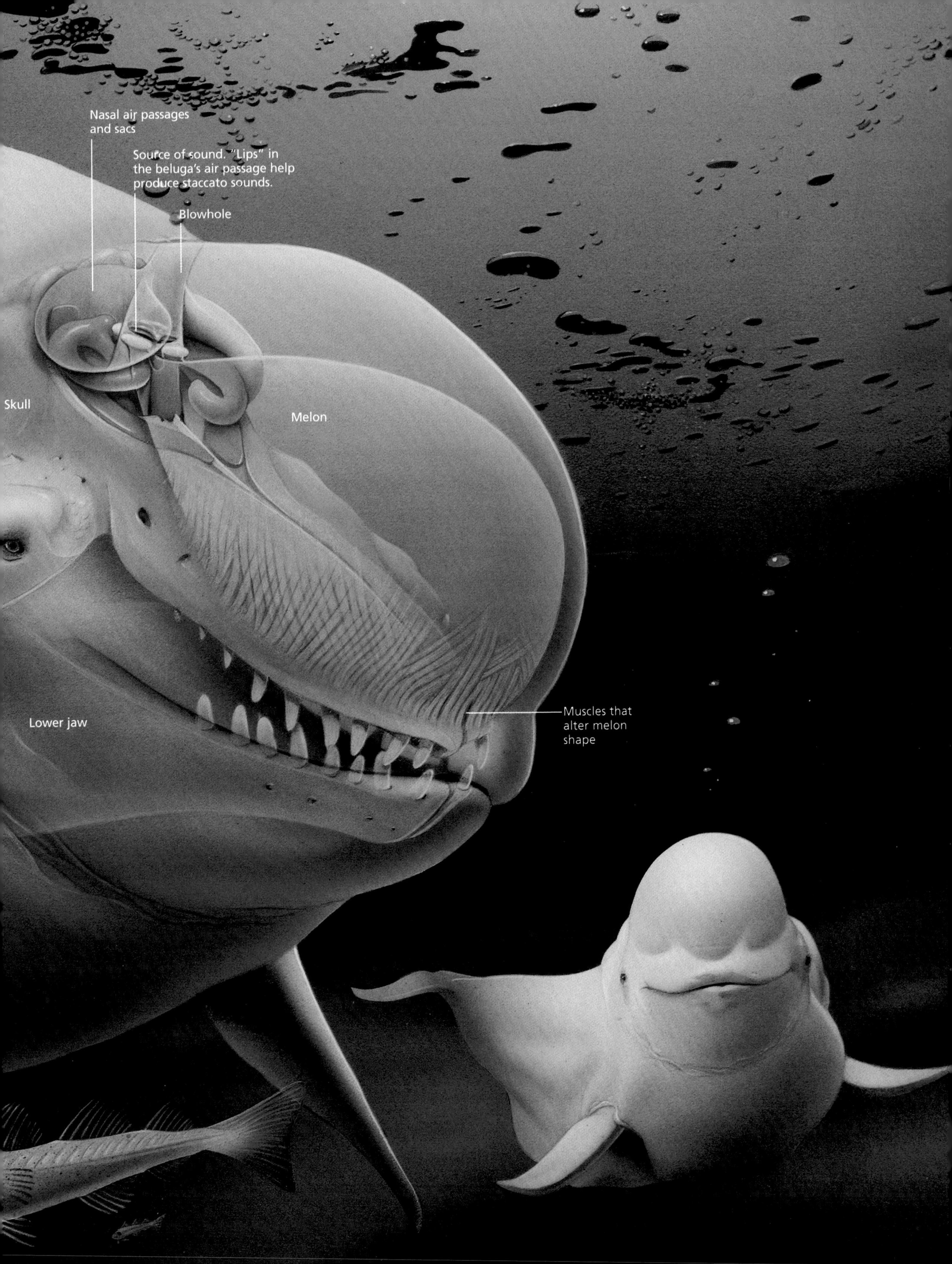

Nasal air passages
and sacs

Source of sound. "Lips" in
the beluga's air passage help
produce staccato sounds.

Blowhole

Skull

Melon

Lower jaw

Muscles that
alter melon
shape

PART III

Unseen Worlds

"We wander through a world of tiny creatures till now unknown, as if it were a newly-discovered continent of our globe." Thus mused a 17th-century Dutch poet about the newly discovered microscope. Yet even with the aid of microscopes and telescopes, we can probe only so far before even our best tools fail us. And we can see into neither the past or the future. As the artwork in this section demonstrates, talented diagram artists can work with scientists to break the barriers of time and space.

As one of the creative forces behind the computer game *Myst*, Chuck Carter used his unbridled imagination to create fantasy worlds. Now, assisted by archaeologists, Carter helps NATIONAL GEOGRAPHIC readers travel in time by rendering accurate depictions of ancient Mexico and Egypt. Jay Matternes and Ned Seidler journey further back in time with their illustrations of human ancestors and prehistoric life. Barron Storey, on the other hand, helps us explore the extremes of the universe. He takes us to a black hole in space, while Jane Hurd shrinks us to germ size for a close-up view of a bacterial menagerie. What a privilege to have these artists as guides to worlds we cannot see. Where our human eyes have failed, their imagination has prevailed.

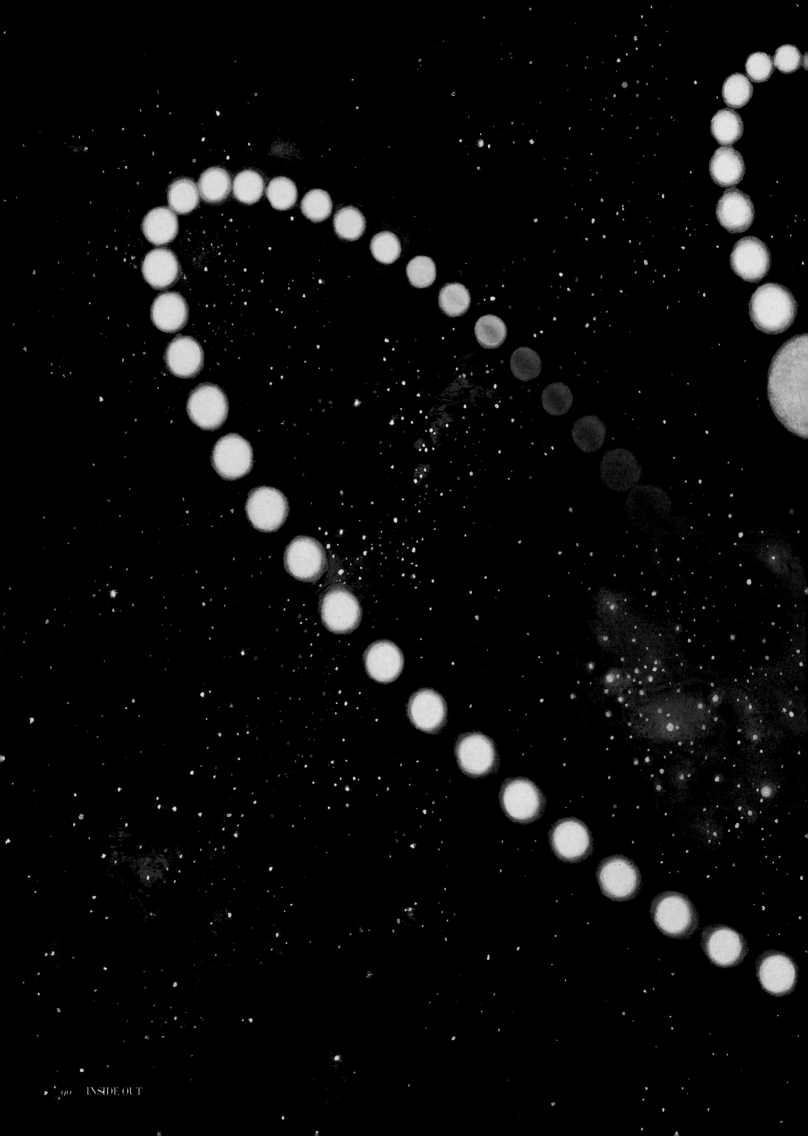

LIFE CYCLE OF A STAR
Illustration by DAVIS MELTZER

"Fiery string of stellar beads depicts the life cycle of the medium-size star that is our sun. Five billion years ago, gravity collapses a nebula, center, far too large to show in true scale. A star forms, its nuclear furnace ignites, and it quickly matures to today's yellow star. Five billion years from now [less the 24 years since this was published], its inner fuel consumed, it expands into a red giant a hundred times its present size. Then it becomes a white dwarf and finally a cinder," explains the 1974 caption.

The life and death of a star has been illustrated in NATIONAL GEOGRAPHIC several times. Barron Story built upon Davis Meltzer's diagram in an update on the same topic—the universe—in 1983. Joe Tucciarone illustrated the birth of a star in a 1995 article on the Orion Nebula. All three artists gave the topic an informative but personalized treatment.

In the 1974 article, this diagram was published as a one-page vertical. Since space has no "up" or "down," the art can work upside down or sideways—a graphic designer's dream.

NATIONAL GEOGRAPHIC—May 1974

THE COCKROACH
Illustration by **PAUL BREEDEN**

"Nothing succeeds like a cockroach when it comes to surviving," the text reads. "Lacking food, a roach can subsist on glue, paper, or soap. With nothing to eat, the American roach in this diagram can draw on body stores, and live as long as three months. It can last a month without water. Lightning-fast responses and receptors sensitive even to another roach's footfall enable cockroaches to thwart a human heel in hot pursuit. They can tolerate many times more radiation than man, perhaps because of their thick body walls, and one species can survive freezing for 48 hours.

"World travelers, roaches have hitchhiked aboard ships, submarines, and planes, thriving everywhere but in the polar regions. The United States harbors about 55 species.

"But this irrepressible insect is a health menace. Roaches carry viruses and bacteria that cause such diseases as hepatitis, polio, typhoid fever, plague, and salmonella, which they may track from one place to another."

Four call-out diagrams accompany the larger roach painting. They provide information on taste hairs, antenna, body wall, and sensory hairs—each magnified 120 to 1500 times life size.

Researcher Merrill Clift visited the Smithsonian's Museum of Natural History for reference material for the artist. She returned with a box of half a dozen cockroaches mounted on pins, on loan from the generous experts. The specimens became models for a line-up drawing, for the same story, of four species that enjoy different parts of your house.

Illustrator Paul Breeden's rich texture and captivating detail, coupled with Howard Paine's elegant page design, achieves the look of a real roach sitting on the page. So remarkable was this cockroach that typographer Charlie Uhl suggested we print it multiple times—on shelf paper.

National Geographic—January 1981

Taste hairs ———

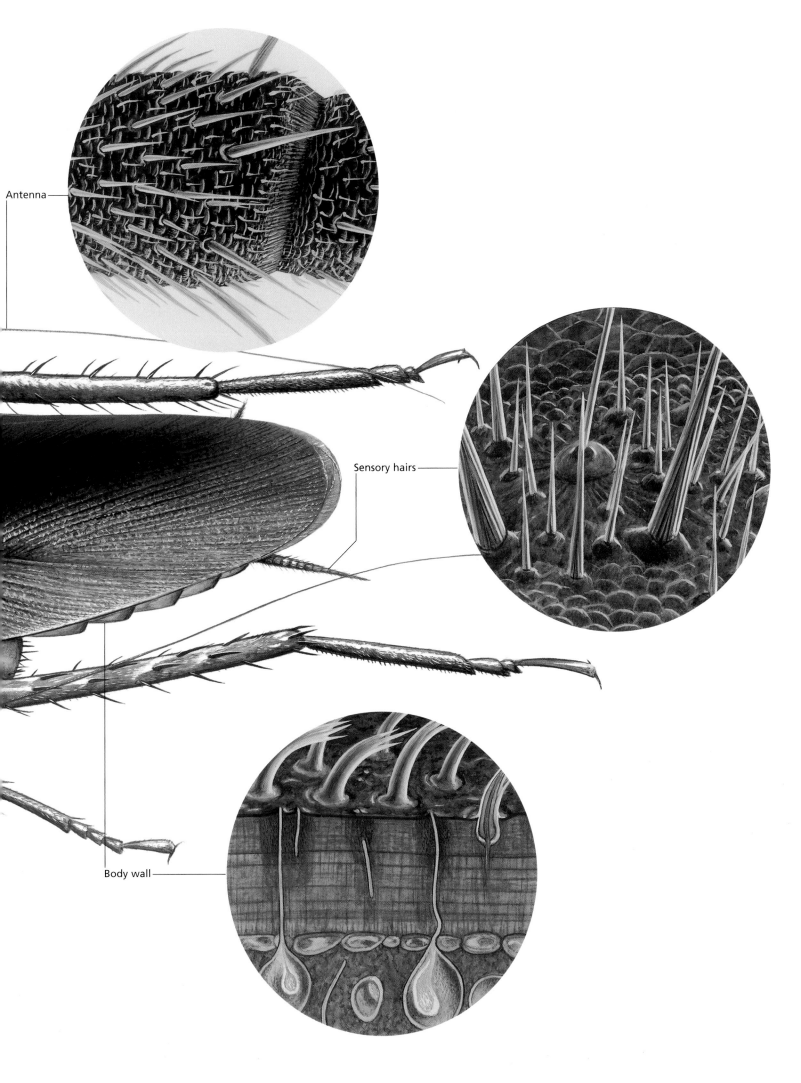

Antenna

Sensory hairs

Body wall

ETHNIC NEIGHBORHOODS OF TEOTIHUACAN

Illustration by CHUCK CARTER

Raising the roof on this barrio of standard housing near the city limits of a great commercial center reveals the hubbub of daily life.

"Mesoamerica's first metropolis, Teotihuacan rivaled Rome in size in the mid-first millennium A.D. Ritual site, marketplace, and art center, it influenced many regions. Centuries after its fall the Aztec called it the Place of the Gods," writes George Stuart, Vice President of the Society and Maya scholar.

"Immigrants from the Veracruz area built the familiar adobe houses of their native Gulf Coast," the text explains. "Distinctive mass burials (1) and abundant foreign pottery (2) were as unusual as the round houses in this area. In addition to processing fibers and weaving (3), this community probably traded in tropical luxuries such as cacao, rubber, and quetzal feathers."

Illustrator Chuck Carter, whose medium is the computer, worked with art director Mark Holmes and researcher David Wooddell to reconstruct the dwelling from the archaeologists' findings, drawings, and analyses. Using a layering technique to define place, an aerial photograph of the modern location forms the background, and a red square marks the location of the building site, called Merchants' Barrio.

Following archaeological evidence precisely is important in making a diagram. The tough questions asked by artists sometimes lead experts to a better understanding of the site.

NATIONAL GEOGRAPHIC—December 1995

Pyramid of the Moon

Pyramid of the Sun

Altar

Washing
textiles

Backstrap-
loom weaving

Drying
yarn

Mass
burial

MERCHANTS'
BARRIO

Spinning
yarn

San
Juan
River

Looted
shaft tomb

1

2

3

3

MOCHE LORD
Illustration by: **NED SEIDLER**

If the police hadn't caught thieves looting a tomb just meters from this Moche lord's final resting place, the wealthiest tomb in the Western Hemisphere would have been lost to archaeologists and to millions of NATIONAL GEOGRAPHIC readers.

The discovery was fresh when the magazine was alerted. Art director Bob Teringo and artist Ned Seidler traveled to the remote Peruvian tomb site and worked out a plan for the art. Seidler's almost unparalleled skill with color, light, and texture took time, especially with the variety of pieces. Details changed, too, since archaeologists were learning more every day.

Even after ongoing archaeology has revealed more burials associated with this *huaca*, or tomb (June 1990), the diagram remains a reference tool, published several times in other publications and hanging in museums.

Regarded as one of the great illustrations published in NATIONAL GEOGRAPHIC, this diagram is the result of masterly technique and execution of a design perfectly suited to the subject. Archaeological analysis of the pieces by Peruvian director Walter Alva and UCLA expert Christopher Donnan was swift and insightful, adding a third dimension to the harmonious balance.

According to the published caption, "the warrior-priest lay surrounded by men and women—even his faithful dog. An area of dirt and rubble surrounded by mud brick suggested that the platform had been opened and resealed after its construction. Twelve feet down, archaeologists came upon the skeleton of a man about 20 years old with a gilded copper helmet and copper shield, whom they dubbed the guardian. Fragments of roofing beams were dated to about A.D. 290. A few feet lower, copper strapping and the imprint of planking mark the warrior-priest's coffin. Buried at his head and feet, two women, about 20, possibly were wives or concubines. Flanking the central coffin lie two men, about 40, one buried with the dog. They lie to the right of the excavated coffin with the other man at left. "

In developing an effective diagram of this complex tomb—or any similar diagram—it is important to understand exactly what is to be explained. "The concept is the most important element," explains art director Bob Teringo. "We had the experts at hand to give us the facts, and we needed to stay focused on what it was we wanted to explain. Seidler's work grew out of one focus—layer upon layer of precious Moche items."

The published caption identifies items buried with the Moche ruler, who was about five feet six inches and in his early 30s, according to skeletal analysis:

1) three-planked lid to the coffin
2) feather ornaments
3) fabric banners with gilded copper platelets
4) 11 pectorals
5) gilded copper headdress
6) textile headband
7) outer shirt of gilded copper platelets
8) head and chest ornaments
9) gold rattle
10) ingots
11) inner white garment
12) bracelets
13) copper knife
14) seashells
15) copper sandals
16) gold headdress ornament
17) crescent-shaped gold bells
18) copper headdress chin strap
19) copper strips
20) three shrouds enfolded everything
21) copper strapping
22) shells, miniature war club and shield
23) copper-pointed atlatl darts
24) guardian
25) warrior-priest's coffin

NATIONAL GEOGRAPHIC—October 1988

PLANET EARTH
Illustration by: **NED SEIDLER**

Chemical precursors

Origins of life

Stromatolites

O_2

Aerobic respiration

Ozone

Eukaryotes

Four billion years ago

Three billion

Two billion

One billion

Masterful solution to a Herculean challenge, this diagram depicts four and a half billion years of geologic and biologic history along a double helix—the structure of DNA, the chemical code for life.

From birth—out of the gas and dust of the early solar system (upper right)—past dinosaurs, like Tyrannosaurus (lower center), to the emergence of modern mammals, Ned Seidler worked his magic in light, shadow, and color.

Allen Carroll's thorough research and meticulous design, teamed with Seidler's precision in oil paint, won them recognition from the Society of Illustrators in 1985. The diagram dealt with complex illustration problems of time and scale—a time frame of 4.5 billion years and a scale that went from the solar system to DNA in a single magazine spread.

Actually, more than a spread was allocated—a double gatefold design gave the diagram needed space. Two numbered line drawings of the upper and lower halves, corresponding to both the text and the art, served to identify the rich layers of information. Accompanying text met the same challenge of space limitation to tell the history of the earth in words.

Time and space were publishing luxuries that NATIONAL GEOGRAPHIC allowed Seidler, who then returned the favor for the education and enjoyment of millions of readers worldwide.

NATIONAL GEOGRAPHIC—August 1985

EXTINCTION

560

Diversification
of animals

500

420

Early
vertebrates

360

Vertebrates
invade the
land

300

Coal swamp
forests

230

MASS
EXTINCTION

180

Dinosaurs

120

Flowering
plants

65

MASS
EXTINCTION

Today

Emergence
of man

MAN-INDUCED
EXTINCTION?

60 million years
from now

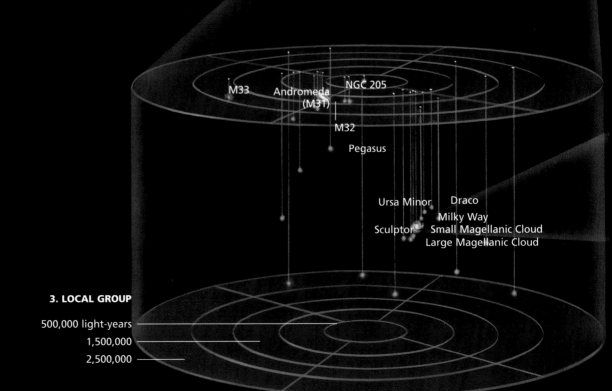

15,000,000,000

20,000,000,000

THE UNIVERSE
Illustration by ROB WOOD

"**E**ven a casual glance at the night sky hints at a universe of stupendous size and beauty. Powerful telescopes scanning the electromagnetic spectrum reveal a cosmos of intricate structure and unimaginable violence. It is a battleground of forces shaping matter and releasing huge quantities of energy that find their way to earth as light and other forms of radiation," explains the text.

Known for authoritative and handsome atlases, the Society found its sixth edition needed important revisions almost immediately after publication due to significant world events that changed country boundaries. The revised atlas also contained a chapter placing the world in a larger context, with this diagram providing a key explanation.

"Cylinders, with grids measured in light-years, show changes in volumes of space. The grids help estimate the distance of celestial objects from an imaginary center, while green drop lines help locate the relative positions of objects within the cylinders," relates the caption.

Included in the diagram is the known universe projected on a flat disk with a radius of 20 billion light-years. Most astronomers estimate the age of the universe to be between 10 and 20 billion years.

National Geographic Atlas of the World, Revised 6th Edition—1992

Sculptor Centaurus

M33 Andromeda NGC 205
(M31)

M32

Pegasus

Ursa Minor Draco
Milky Way
Sculptor Small Magellanic Cloud
Large Magellanic Cloud

3. LOCAL GROUP

500,000 light-years

1,500,000

2,500,000

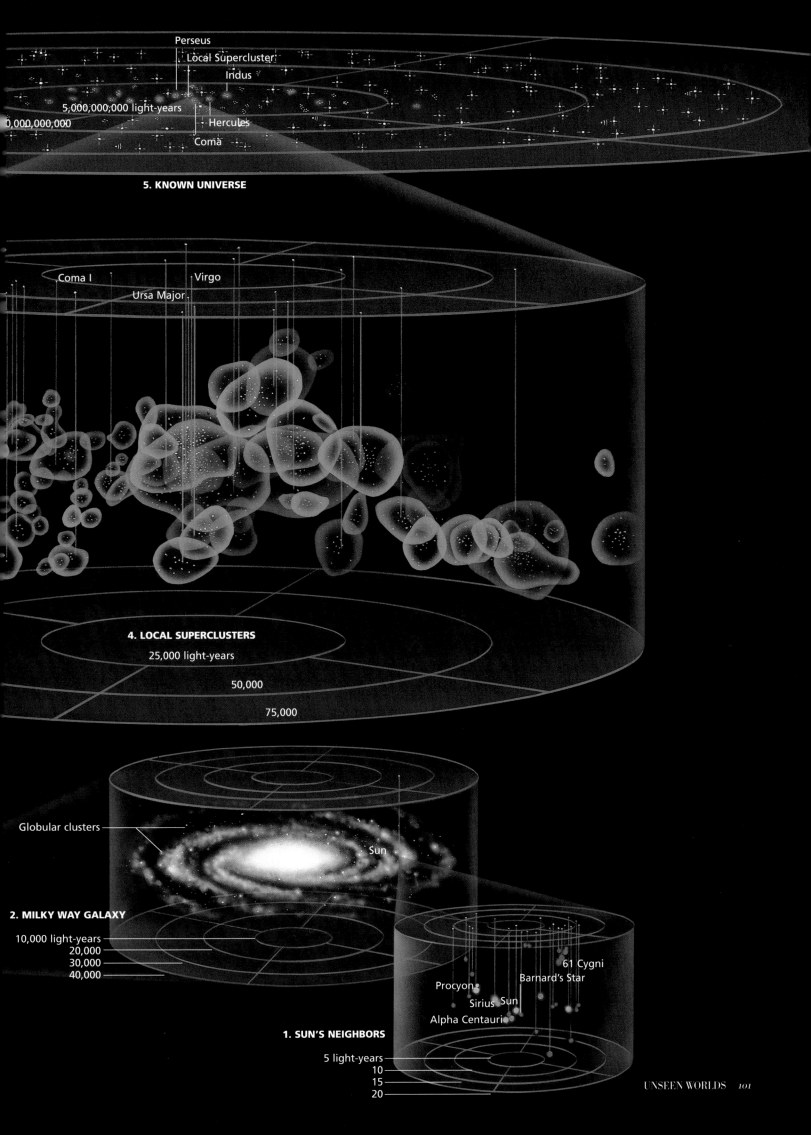

5. KNOWN UNIVERSE

Perseus

Local Supercluster

Indus

5,000,000,000 light-years

0,000,000,000

Hercules

Coma

4. LOCAL SUPERCLUSTERS

Coma I

Virgo

Ursa Major

25,000 light-years

50,000

75,000

2. MILKY WAY GALAXY

Globular clusters

Sun

10,000 light-years
20,000
30,000
40,000

1. SUN'S NEIGHBORS

61 Cygni

Barnard's Star

Procyon

Sirius Sun

Alpha Centauri

5 light-years
10
15
20

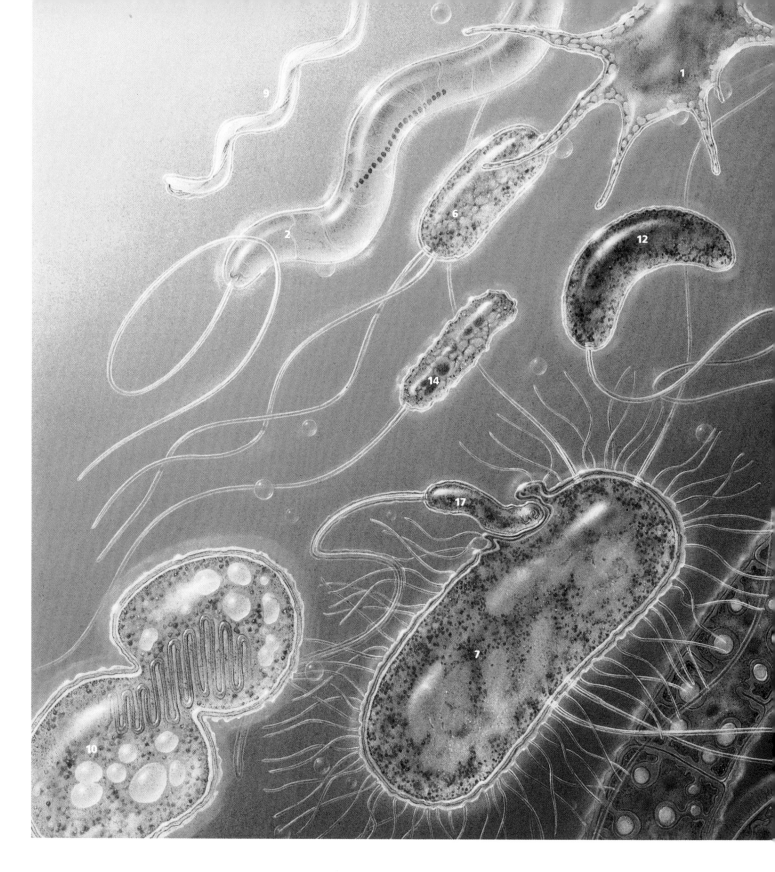

BACTERIA
Illustration by JANE HURD

Like a family photograph album, this portrait offers clues for identifying bacteria. Illustrator Jane Hurd conveys an idealized form of these microscopic organisms. With her knowledge of different types of microscopy, Hurd worked with experts and art researcher Hillel Hoffmann to define the key characteristics of each bacterium. Sifting through vast amounts of information, deciding on the most important elements, and then visually accentuating those few key traits is the skill of a medical or science illustrator.

Scale was another challenge. With different magnifications for different bacteria, Hurd and art director Allen Carroll agreed on a scheme that increases the size of the bacteria in the front and decreases the

size of the bacteria in back so that all are in proportion. The artist chose the blue and green hues to reflect the "sea" of bacteria she imagined.

As the published caption states, "Nature's most diverse life-form, bacteria have adapted to almost every environmental niche. Some, like *Ancalochloris* (1), *Aquaspirillum* (2), and *Chromatium* (3) live in water, where *Aquaspirillum* may use its magnetic particle chain to find food-rich sediment. *Haloarcula* (4) thrives in salty places. *Pyrodictium* (5) seeks hot spots. *Rhizobium* (6) colonizes plant roots and produces a form of nitrogen vital to its host. Other types of bacteria, including *Escherichia* (7), *Streptococcus* (8), and *Treponema* (9), can cause disease in humans.

"Metabolic needs sometimes bring together disparate species. *Methylococcus* (10), an aerobic methane consumer, may be drawn to *Methanosarcina* (11), an anaerobic methane producer; *Desulfovibrio* (12), a hydrogen sulfide producer, attracts *Ancalochloris, Beggiatoa* (13), and *Chromatium,* which consume that compound.

"Another group of hydrogen sulfide consumers, *Thiobacillus* (14), helps leach metals like copper from ore. *Streptomyces* (15) makes antibiotics. *Anabaena* (16) produces oxygen from water during photo-synthesis, while *Bdellovibrio* (17) attacks many other bacteria."

NATIONAL GEOGRAPHIC—August 1993

QUASARS AND BLACK HOLES

Illustration by **BARRON STOREY**

Like a professor's blackboard, this diagram explains the complex theory of black holes in space. Exceedingly odd, but perhaps relatively common, black holes may be scattered across the universe in a variety of sizes. A rotating black hole of 100 million solar masses with a diameter equal to Mars's orbit could be a powerful engine. Here, such an engine drives the quasar at the heart of a young galaxy.

Barron Storey is a mentor for many other artists. He possesses an outstanding ability to communicate creatively what is in his mind's eye. In this diagram, with the art direction of Jan Adkins, he handles the difficult scale problem related to universe diagrams with a red locator square and progressively magnified views. Also for this story, he created a dynamic and innovative design to tell the history of the universe.

Finished diagrams frequently need to be corrected due to errors identified by researchers or design changes by editors. Before computer scans and inexpensive overnight delivery were common, last-minute changes were made by staff artist Bill Bond (see Pinatubo, pages 24-25). Often asked to copy an artist's style to correct minor inaccuracies, Bill accomplished seamless alterations that are nearly impossible to detect. Most of the original artists would trust only Bill with their work. In this case, due to information acquired close to the print deadline, Bill clarified the "confused magnetic field" of this black hole.

NATIONAL GEOGRAPHIC—June 1983

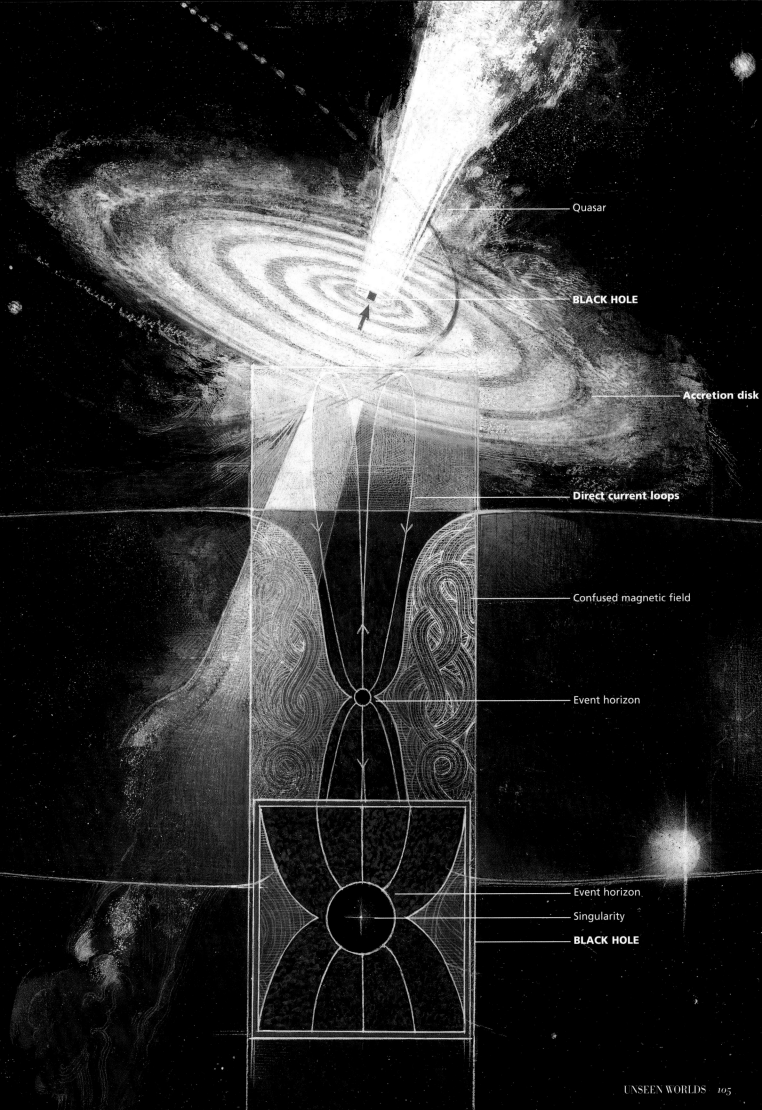

Quasar

BLACK HOLE

Accretion disk

Direct current loops

Confused magnetic field

Event horizon

Event horizon

Singularity

BLACK HOLE

SKULL 1470
Illustration by **JAY MATTERNES**

"All those old bones look alike," is the lament of many non-scientists. Addressing the readership's curiosity and lack of background information, artist and naturalist Jay Matternes's diagram is a step-by-step primer. Published in 1973, the diagram is still a useful resource, even in a field where knowledge is continually updated.

The legendary Leakey family's long association with the Society included the announcement of the discovery of Skull 1470. Text for the art described the process: "Combining known anatomical facts with well-informed speculation, Matternes reconstructs a likeness of '1470 man.' On the far left, the reconstructed skull had a cranial capacity measuring some 800 cubic centimeters. This is little more than half modern man's, but significantly larger than that of *Australopithecus*— the hominid roaming East Africa at the same time as '1470 man.'

"To the bare bone, artist Matternes adds teeth, lower jaw, and other missing skeletal fragments—shaded dark brown (second from left). Teeth found with fragments of a second skull provided a basis for the lower jaw's reconstruction. Jaw and molars of *Australopithecus* were more massive, suggesting a diet of coarse vegetation. Those of the second specimen—still somewhat larger than ours—imply a mixed diet of raw foods, including meat.

"The artist adds eyes, fatty tissue, cartilage, and underlying musculature (third from left). Note the absence of the apelike "beetle brow" of *Australopithecus* and such later creatures as *Homo erectus*. (An illustrated time line published in the story provided a comparison of skull shapes.)

"Adding ears, more cartilage, eyebrows, and lips, plus salivary glands, superficial muscles, and fatty tissue, the artist approaches the finished portrait (largest)."

With flesh attached (far right), the completed "1470 man" may have been a woman. Without the post-cranial remains, Leakey could not be sure. This head drawing was published alongside a drawing of the grasslands, delta, and forested landscape inhabited by "1470 Person."

National Geographic—June 1973

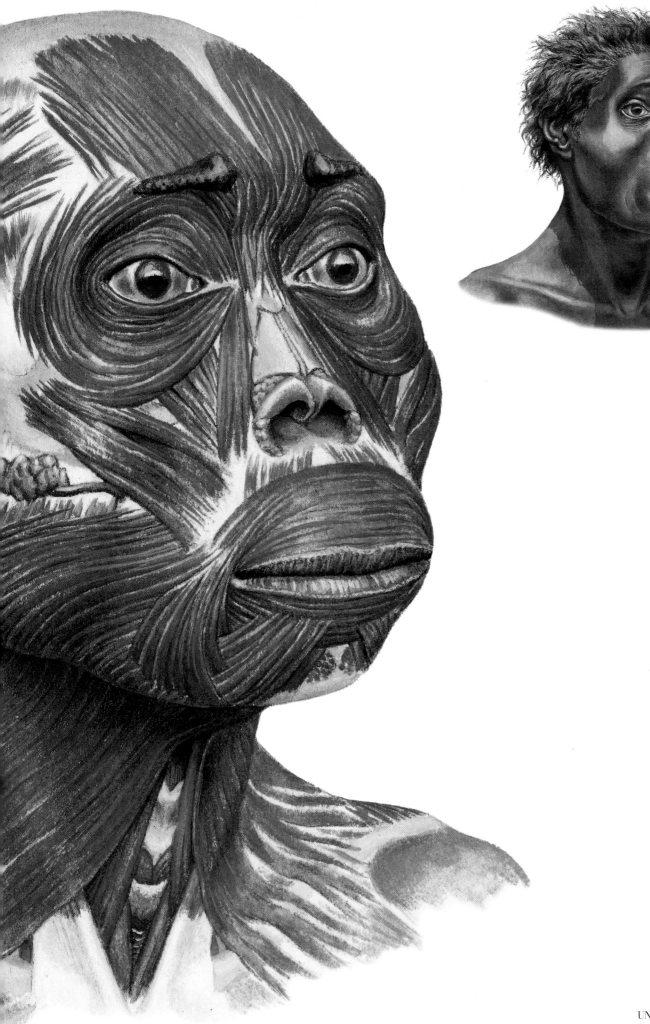

JELLYFISH
(TOXIC DART GUN)
Illustration by ED GAZSI

Swimming in tropical waters off the northern coast of Australia can be a deadly experience when box jellyfish are in the neighborhood.

Underwater specialist David Doubilet photographed the Australian habitat and beautiful portraits of the sea creature engaged in eating or being eaten, as well as victims of its torturous sting. This diagram, with accompanying published text, explains the life cycle of the box jellyfish and also shows how it penetrates a swimmer's foot.

"A life span of only months begins after ova and sperm unite. A planula (1) develops into a polyp (2) that attaches to the underside of a rock. Reproducing asexually, creeping polyps (3) shed new polyps, here resembling arms. Final shape comes with metamorphosis (4) into a young medusa (5), from which an adult (6) emerges."

Artist Ed Gazsi likes to use Polaroid negatives for reference—here of a human foot and ankle—that result in an appropriately dramatic and somber mood. This diagram indicates the passage of time with five call-out circles. Invisible to the naked eye, but magnified in the circle to the lower right, Gazsi shows the deadly mechanism of the jellyfish.

NATIONAL GEOGRAPHIC—August 1994

6

Human skin tissue

— Capillary

RAIN FOREST CANOPY
Illustration by JOHN DAWSON

Branching out in four directions of study, animals, vascular plants, nonvascular plants, and soil and detritus of the rain forest canopy are illustrated. Photography and text for the story covered "a new breed of scientist who risks life and limb to probe the great unexplored world at the top of tropical rain forests."

Snakes, frogs, birds, mammals, and insects are among the canopy animals (top) visible when the branch is stripped of foliage.

Vascular plants (middle), including bromeliads, ferns, and other epiphytes live here as well.

Nonvascular plants (bottom) like mosses and lichens that spread like a carpet are among the first to colonize the limb.

Illustrator John Dawson, with art director Nick Kirilloff and researcher Hillel Hoffmann, portrayed the complexity of life in the canopy by peeling it back, one layer at a time. Guidance from experts made it possible.

NATIONAL GEOGRAPHIC—December 1991

THE LIVING SOIL
Illustration by NED SEIDLER

"Vast and teeming continents in breadth, mere feet in depth—soil pulses with life," the text caption states. "From microbes to small mammals, plants and animals enrich soil as they live and die.

"Worms feed the moles (far right), whose tunnels serve as soil highways for many species. Moles and other burrowers, like the shrew eating the beetle (near, opposite), and the sleeping ground squirrel (below opposite), help to mix the soil as they tunnel in all directions.

"Nematodes, mites, and springtails (enlarged square) live on the threshold of visibility. Among a farmer's worst pests, nematodes are preyed on by fungi, which snare them with tiny tendrils. In the microcosm (lens), bacteria are the great decomposers in most soils, while fungi prefer acidic conditions."

"Look—up top—a rusty nail for scale," reflects art director Howard Paine. "You can look at Ned's paintings superficially, or you can explore them like a child. Children pore over visuals, and Ned gives all ages something to discover when you look at his paintings."

Patient attention to every hair of his shrews and moles has made Seidler a legend—building, with every diagram, the GEOGRAPHIC's reputation as the place to see what usually can't be seen.

NATIONAL GEOGRAPHIC—September 1984

Bacteria
and fungi

Nematodes,
mites, and springtails

SKYSCRAPERS
Illustration by WILLIAM H. BOND

An architect's lineup of the major skyscrapers of the United States shows architectural trends over time. The Washington Monument in Washington, D.C., completed in 1885, marks the beginning of the comparison on the left, and AT&T headquarters, completed in 1984, marks the end on the far right.

The caption for the artwork reads: "Tall, taller, tallest became attributes of modern buildings after the advent of the safe passenger elevator in 1852 made higher stories easily accessible and iron framing (later steel and reinforced concrete) made them stable. But the name skyscraper wasn't applied until the 1880s. The skyscraper developed simultaneously in Chicago and in New York and has since changed the face of cities across America."

Artist Bill Bond (see Pinatubo, pages 24-25) worked as a staff artist for NATIONAL GEOGRAPHIC magazine for 29 years before retiring. But retiring meant doing work for additional clients, including the Society's Book Division. Bond's architectural renderings include the Old Post Office Building in Washington, D.C., the Washington National Cathedral, and a prototype painting of the National Geographic Society's M Street building addition before it was completed in 1984.

NATIONAL GEOGRAPHIC—February 1989

Washington Monument

Montauk Block

Tacoma Building

Auditorium Building

Rand McNally Building

Monadnock Building

Reliance Building

Flatiron Building

Ingalls Building

Woolworth Building

Chrysler Building

RCA Building

Empire State Building

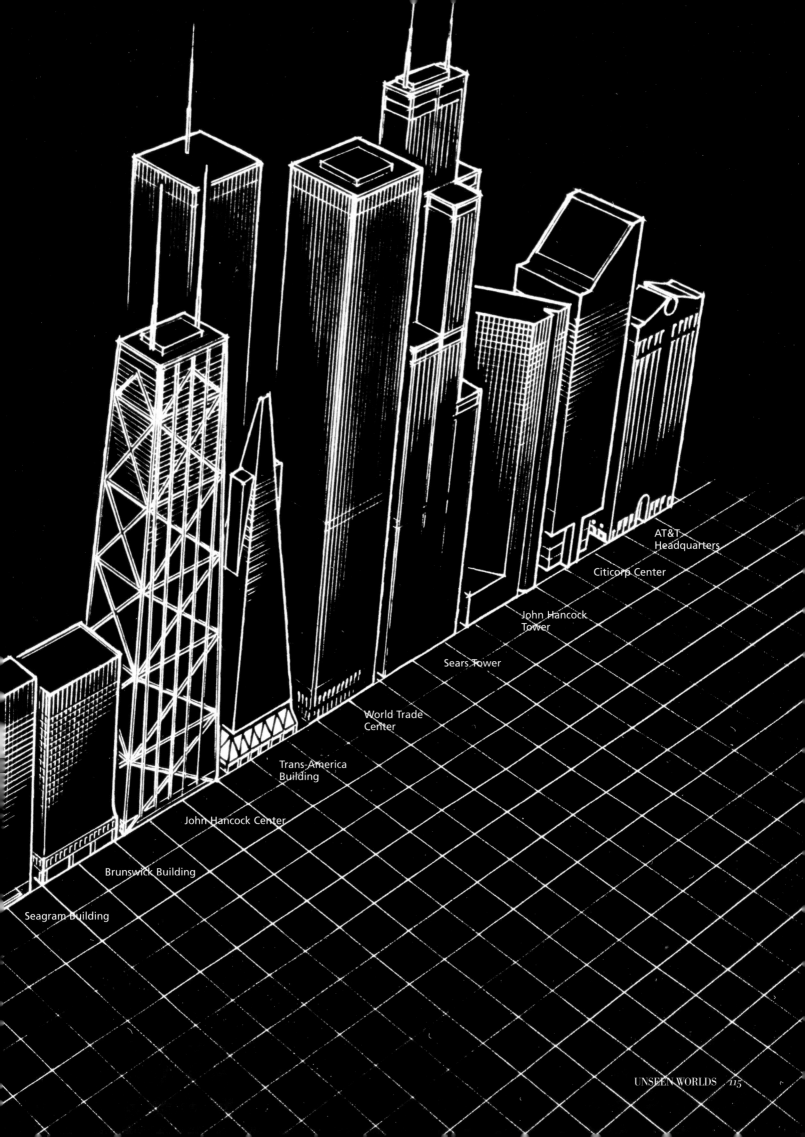

AT&T
Headquarters

Citicorp Center

John Hancock
Tower

Sears Tower

World Trade
Center

Trans-America
Building

John Hancock Center

Brunswick Building

Seagram Building

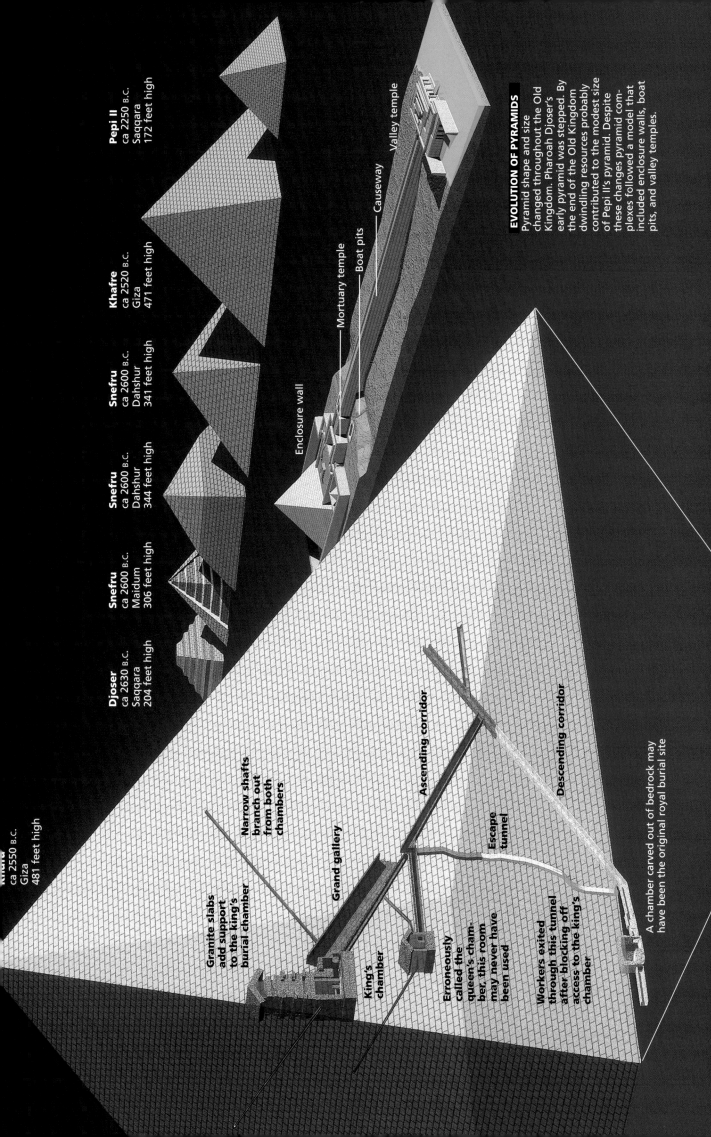

Khufu
ca 2550 B.C.
Giza
481 feet high

Djoser
ca 2630 B.C.
Saqqara
204 feet high

Snefru
ca 2600 B.C.
Maidum
306 feet high

Snefru
ca 2600 B.C.
Dahshur
344 feet high

Snefru
ca 2600 B.C.
Dahshur
341 feet high

Khafre
ca 2520 B.C.
Giza
471 feet high

Pepi II
ca 2250 B.C.
Saqqara
172 feet high

Enclosure wall

Mortuary temple

Boat pits

Causeway

Valley temple

EVOLUTION OF PYRAMIDS
Pyramid shape and size changed throughout the Old Kingdom. Pharoah Djoser's early pyramid was stepped. By the end of the Old Kingdom dwindling resources probably contributed to the modest size of Pepi II's pyramid. Despite these changes pyramid complexes followed a model that included enclosure walls, boat pits, and valley temples.

Granite slabs add support to the king's burial chamber

Narrow shafts branch out from both chambers

Grand gallery

Ascending corridor

King's chamber

Erroneously called the queen's chamber, this room may never have been used

Escape tunnel

Workers exited through this tunnel after blocking off access to the king's chamber

Descending corridor

A chamber carved out of bedrock may have been the original royal burial site

Illustration by CHUCK CARTER

E arly forays into computer-generated artwork for NATIONAL GEOGRAPHIC magazine were led by freelance Chuck Carter. Art director Chris Sloan hired Carter to depict the unseen world of the pyramids of Egypt's Old Kingdom. Noted Egyptologist Dr. Mark Lehner and other scholars vigilantly kept watch over factual details.

Chris Sloan traveled on assignment to Egypt with photographer Ken Garrett, illustrations editor Elie Rogers, and writer David Roberts. Their work there included re-creating the ancient bread-making technology as well as climbing the Great Pyramid. Access to Egyptian antiquities is necessarily limited but is granted to the Society because of its wide readership and its dedication to accuracy.

Climbing to 481 feet enabled Garrett to produce a panoramic photograph of the modern city. The climb inspired Chris Sloan to design a diagram that answers the question: How did the pharaoh's tomb economically affect so large an area?

Trademark symbol of Egypt's Old Kingdom, the Great Pyramid at Giza forms the cornerstone of the diagram. Although the pyramids are of archaeological interest themselves, recent excavations in adjacent villages, workers' shops, and tombs also yield important information on daily life in the Old Kingdom.

"This story on Egypt's Old Kingdom is a survey story. Traveling to the region put information in context and allowed me to develop a focus for art," explains Sloan.

NATIONAL GEOGRAPHIC—January 1995

Khafre's Pyramid

Workers' Village

Sphinx

Khufu's Great Pyramid

CAIRO

Giza Plateau

Former floodplain

Saqqara

Probable course of Nile in Old Kingdom

Dahshur

Modern channel of Nile

E G Y P T

Nile Delta

AREA ENLARGED ABOVE

Maidum

Nile River

COPÁN ACROPOLIS

Illustration by
CHRISTOPHER A. KLEIN

Copán's towering acropolis, civic and ceremonial heart of a city-state of 20,000 people, took shape during four centuries of construction that began about A.D. 400. Each ruler tore down parts of earlier buildings, some reconstructed here in cutaways, and put his own on top.

"They created a sacred geography," says project director Bill Fash of Harvard University. "You could walk through all the myths of Maya civilization: the Bat House, the House of Knives, the Mountain Where Maize Was Born."

Barbara Fash, of the Peabody Museum at Harvard University, consulted with artist Chris Klein on the visual interpretation of the archaeological work. Their collaboration over the last several years has kept NATIONAL GEOGRAPHIC readers up-to-date on information learned at Copán.

NATIONAL GEOGRAPHIC—December 1997

Structure 16

Rosalila

Newly discovered tombs

Bat House

Mountain
Where Maize
Was Born

Sub-Jaguar
tomb

East Court

House of
Knives

In the Field
at Copán, Honduras

Beneath the ruined temples and plazas of Copán are hundreds of feet of tunnels where archaeologists (below) joined artist Chris Klein (opposite) in an effort to reconstruct the past.

KENNETH GARRETT (BELOW AND OPPOSITE)

CHRISTOPHER A. KLEIN

FROM ABOVE, the Maya ruins at Copán, Honduras, are a confusing jumble of wet stone blocks. Rain forest invades the site from all directions. The ancient temple complex is overrun with jungle. In his mind's eye, artist Chris Klein sees something different.

These are buildings Klein knows intimately as the "Bat House," the "House of Knives," and others with pet names archaeologists have assigned them. He can see past the rubble of today and visualize the ancient inhabitants making smoky sacrifices to their gods from brightly decorated temples and plazas. He knows this place because he has been here three times for NATIONAL GEOGRAPHIC.

Sole staff artist at the NATIONAL GEOGRAPHIC, Klein got his start 19 years ago, painting relief maps and small images for the cartographic division. His illustrations caught the eye of former Art Director Howard Paine, who hired him to work in the magazine's art department.

The Society had supported archaeologists Bill and Barbara Fash in their excavations at Copán since 1979. The Fashes had recently discovered an older temple—nicknamed Rosalila—under the stones of a later structure. Klein's assignment was to render Rosalila's complex structure in art.

On his initial trip, his first to a tropical country, Klein was unprepared for the working conditions at Copán—90°F and high humidity. The only way to understand the architecture of Copán is to crawl into the anthill of tunnels the Maya built under the temple complex. In those tunnels, the temperature drops a little, but the humidity is all consuming. "It's tough trying to use pencil and paper down there when you're dripping all over it," says Klein. "I rely on a camera a lot, but even that's slippery."

"When I go into the tunnels with a scientist, I know we have only an hour, because we can't stand to be in there any longer than that," says Klein. "We visit a specific area with archaeological drawings. The purpose is to get a sense of scale and orientation, but the tunnels are cramped and dark. Working in dim light, it's easy to get disoriented because the tunnels go every which way."

The hardest part of this project for the artist was to put together a mental picture of the structure. "You can never see the whole temple," says Klein,

ESTRUCTURA
11

WEST

CHRISTOPHER A. KLEIN

because the archaeologists haven't exposed the whole building—just bits and pieces here and there. "You just squat in a tunnel and try to visualize how it all fits together. At Copán this is particularly hard because the Maya would put one building right on top of another. They made all kinds of crazy additions too—sort of like adding lots of decks and gazebos to your house."

Like many archaeologists, the Fashes had received art training, and could understand Klein's drawing efforts and give helpful comments. Barbara Fash, in particular, offered pencil drawings of structural details with indications of appropriate color.

Klein's first diagram of Rosalila at Copán was printed in 1991. Little did he know he would be returning four years later to paint that building again. Archaeologists discovered even older temples under Rosalila. New excavations in the tunnels revealed royal burials in the older temples, possibly the tombs of Copán's first rulers. Klein's return assignment to Copán was to paint not only a new version of Rosalila but also the ruins called the "acropolis," which included large plazas, stairways, and other temples.

Since Klein's last visit, archaeologists had produced a full-size replica of

KENNETH GARRETT

Rosalila at a museum in a nearby town. This allowed the artist to check his original sketches against their model and make adjustments. He also had access to new color information.

Color often proves to be one of the most controversial aspects of painted archaeological reconstructions. Paint is one of the first things that disappears from a building over time, and after hundreds of years of weathering, any adhering paint is limited to a few discolored flakes here and there. Although it is known that the Maya painted their buildings extensively, their colors are highly speculative.

Scientists have sophisticated techniques for determining the color of ancient paint, but it is quite a leap between saying "This paint chip was bright red" to "This whole building was bright red." An artist, nevertheless, has to assign a color to everything he or she paints. One of Klein's tasks is to tease color guesses out of the experts, an endeavor that makes them squirm.

The colors of the lively sculptural facades not only changed from Klein's prior illustration but also continued to change as his new work progressed. At first, he was told that the top of the temple was white. Ultimately, Dr. Ricardo Agurcia Fasquelle of the Honduran Institute of Anthropology and History, co-director of excavations at Copán, informed Klein that the top of the temple was actually very colorful.

One color issue was so controversial that it prompted Klein to take his questions to an archeology symposium on the Maya held at Harvard University. At issue was the color of the plaza surface in his cutaway diagram of the Copán acropolis. By presenting his painting to a group of top experts there, Klein helped them arrive at a consensus. They were able to agree that the plaza surface was cream-colored, not red. Unfortunately, this meant that he had to repaint all the plazas.

One mark of a NATIONAL GEOGRAPHIC artist is to take such last minute changes in stride. "Often experts don't make good comments when they're reviewing art until they see the final painting in color," Klein says. "I wish they'd catch things earlier, but the most important thing is that we get it right in the end."

—*Chris Sloan*

New discoveries at Copán made it possible for the artist to sketch the location of new burial sites (opposite, upper) and for museum workers to reconstruct the temple facade (opposite, lower). Klein reviewed his artwork at every stage with archaeologists (above).

Rosalila

Royal female burial

Margarita

Royal male burial

STRUCTURE 16

About the Illustrators

The illustrators whose work is included in this book have diverse talents and interests but, at heart, they have many characteristics in common. By nature curious and inquisitive, illustrators think visually and tend to dive into research and problem-solving. Above all, illustrators are storytellers.

Harry Bliss

When a German calligrapher encouraged Bliss to become an artist after seeing his sketches of American soldiers during World War II, he listened. Captivated by "creating something out of nothing," Bliss took up art as a career.

He has earned awards from *Communication Arts* magazine, the Illustrators Annual, the 1990 "Communicator of the Year" award, as well as many local awards. After working for Great Lakes Press, the Dixie Cup Company, and Studio 5 (as part owner) he operated his own illustration studio from 1973-1986. Currently, his work is widely exhibited. Bliss has taught watercolor and design at the Rochester Institute of Technology. He has also taught illustration and design at Graphic Careers. His two sons are artists too. The *Peoples and Places of the Past* assignment resulted from a spontaneous visit to see his friend NATIONAL GEOGRAPHIC art director Bob Teringo, who immediately put Bliss to work on the project.

William H. Bond

As a signalman in the British Royal Navy, Bond was part of the invasion forces that landed on Sicily and in Salerno to establish onshore visual communications in 1943. Fifty years later, he illustrated the fifty United States Postal Service World War II commemorative stamps, issued in five sheets. The third sheet depicted his year in the Mediterranean. From 1966 until his retirement in 1995, Bond served as a staff artist at NATIONAL GEOGRAPHIC magazine. In addition to numerous magazine stories, he was assigned to special projects, including painting the mountains of land and of the ocean floor for a physical world globe as well as nine spreads of flora and fauna for the Society's *Atlas of North America*. When the Society built a new building in 1984, Bond made corrections to a painting of the night sky on a dome in the entrance foyer.

Retirement led to freelance work for NATIONAL GEOGRAPHIC magazine and other Society publications and to portrait painting.

Paul Breeden

For ten years, Breeden created fine drawings, realistic renderings, and calligraphy for NATIONAL GEOGRAPHIC. Other magazines that have commissioned his wildlife paintings are *Audubon, Sierra, Defenders of Wildlife, Reader's Digest*, and *Ranger Rick*.

Breeden illustrated Peter Jenkins's best-selling book *A Walk Across America*. He also illustrated 24 volumes for the "Lost Civilizations" series published by Time-Life Books. The pine cone postage stamp was Breeden's commission from the U.S. Postal Service. He also served on the staff of the White House calligrapher.

The Breedens run Spring Woods Gallery in Sullivan, Maine, where Paul's recent work of earth-inspired compositions can be seen.

Allen Carroll

Carroll is managing director of National Geographic Maps and senior vice president of National Geographic Enterprises, a for-profit subsidiary of the Society begun in 1996.

He began his career as a freelance illustrator. His clients included the *Washington Post, Smithsonian* magazine, the *New Republic* and the Johns Hopkins University.

Carroll joined the art department of NATIONAL GEOGRAPHIC magazine in 1983. His creative visualizations using computer or color pencil launched the magazine's modern use of diagrams to explain complex scientific theories.

Often teased for his obvious obsession with arrows, Carroll hopes someone will invite him to lecture on the design and use of these diagrammatic tools.

Chuck Carter

A self-taught illustrator, Carter began creating informational graphics and feature illustrations for a variety of newspapers using pen and ink and watercolor. His interest in using computers for 3-D modeling began at the *Spokesman-Review* in Spokane, Washington. Knight-Ridder hired him to design portraits that were distributed internationally via Presslink, their computer bulletin board. He provided animated news graphics to TV stations around the world through Knight-Ridder's "News In Motion" project.

Carter designed graphics for the CD-ROM game *Myst*, produced by a small company named Cyan. Freelance work included his innovative diagrams for NATIONAL GEOGRAPHIC magazine as well as animation and illustrations for the Society's award-winning Web site (www.nationalgeographic.com).

Currently working at Westwood Studios in Las Vegas, Nevada, Carter designs art and animation for a variety of games.

John Dawson

Living on the Big Island of Hawaii with its lush tropical rain forests has enhanced naturalist John Dawson's expertise in natural history illustration. He has illustrated the variety of Hawaii's flora and fauna for several NATIONAL GEOGRAPHIC articles.

Dawson's work is also commissioned by the National Wildlife Federation, National Park Service, and U.S. Postal Service.

For a 1984 NATIONAL GEOGRAPHIC magazine article on ants, Dawson painted 20 illustrations of ants and their behavior under the guidance of ant expert Bert Höldobler and Art Director Howard Paine.

Dawson has illustrated several books, including *The Grand Canyon: An Artist's View* with writer Charles Craighead. An earlier book, *A Naturalist's Notebook*, reflects field sketchbooks he makes during getaways to the woods.

Dawson's wife Kathleen does research for his work. They continue to collaborate with Charles Craighead on children's book projects.

Don Foley

Foley has won more than two dozen regional, national, and international awards for informational graphics and design work in the fast-paced newspaper world. Clients include the *New York Times*, Gannett, and Knight-Ridder. His two books, *Animation and 3D Modeling on the Mac* and *Animation Tips and Tricks for Windows and Mac* are popular instructional works. As adjunct faculty at Northern Virginia Community College, Foley teaches 3-D modeling techniques. Currently, he is a freelance illustrator and animator providing "information-based imagery."

Edward S. Gazsi

Gazsi's letterhead design depicts an eyeball with an arm drawing what it sees in a mirror—the service he provides. His trained eye in illustration won him a gold medal from the Society of Illustrators in New York in 1988. His clients include many book and magazine publishers.

Gazsi earned a B.F.A. degree from the Cooper Union for the Advancement of Arts and Sciences in New York City and also studied under Philip Pearlstein at Brooklyn College.

He teaches drawing, human anatomy, and illustration techniques at the International Academy of Merchandising and Design in Tampa, Florida, as well as in many public speaking venues.

Gazsi lives with his family in Bayonet Point, Florida, where he is currently working on his fourth illustrated children's book.

Dale Gustafson

Gustafson has worked for literally hundreds of companies in virtually every field of industry and publishing. His biographical summary includes a client list of seven categories with a dozen clients per category, ranging from breweries to airlines to auto parts. He specializes in technical subjects, cutaways, and exploded diagrams.

After a year in the Navy at the end of World War II, Gustafson graduated from Pomona College and the Art Center School of Design. He studied industrial and automotive design on a scholarship from General Motors. After illustrating cars for Buick, GM, Pontiac, and Opel for the first 17 years of his career, Gustafson became a freelance illustrator in the 1970s. He is represented by Mendola, Ltd. in New York City.

Greg Harlin

Harlin graduated from the University of Georgia with a B.F.A. in graphic design. For more than 16 years, he has worked with the design and illustration firm Wood Ronsaville Harlin where he has created illustrations for a number of national magazines and book publishers in addition to the NATIONAL GEOGRAPHIC, including *Smithsonian, Reader's Digest*, Time-Life Books, and *Air and Space*. He has received recognition from *Communication Arts* magazine and the Society of Illustrators.

Harlin works in Annapolis, Maryland, a short drive from the Society's headquarters in Washington, D.C. Art directors and researchers enjoy getting out of the office to join Harlin at the WRH studio, where they pose for artist reference figures in a wide variety of period costumes and wigs.

Karel Havlicek

Havlicek is amazed that his friends from the 1970s and 80s in Prague—where he received his art training—are in the Czech government today. His friends were dissidents who opposed the communist government. When the secret police forced Havlicek to choose between his decade-long friendships and his citizenship, he lost his passport—and everything. "A citizen of the world, with no citizenship," he recalls. After two years in Austria he moved to California where his work caught the attention of NATIONAL GEOGRAPHIC Art Director Howard Paine.

Havlicek's clients now include Banana Republic, the Nature Conservancy, and Honda. California is still his address, although his passion for collecting and growing tropical plants makes his home look like Hawaii.

Jane Hurd

Hurd operates her own illustration and graphics studio, where she specializes in medical animation using 3-D and 2-D software. Hurd art directed the design for the launch of the PBS magazine show *HealthWeek*, and continues to produce its medical animations.

Hurd developed the graphic look of the Time-Life medical videotapes on the 30 most prevalent diseases, written for patients. The series, containing 90 minutes of her full 3-D animation, has won more than 50 national and international awards.

Hurd earned her B.S. in medical art from the University of Illinois Medical Center. For 13 years, from her studio in Bethesda, Maryland, she created medical illustrations for patient, public, and physician education as well as for advertising. She now lives in Brooklyn, New York.

Keith Kasnot

As a certified medical illustrator, Kasnot has worked on a number of film, multi-image, and exhibition projects in addition to editorial illustration.

His animations have appeared in PBS documentaries such as NOVA and the BBC's *Horizon* series. As creative director of the Arizona Heart Institute's VAS Communications, he produced "A Celebration of the Heart," using 33 carousels and 2,400 slides.

Kasnot's work and his technique have been highlighted in *Step-by-Step Graphics*, *Print* magazine, and other publications.

It was his wife, a physical therapist, who first suggested he study medical illustration after he had begun a Master's degree in sculpture. He earned a Master's in biomedical communications from the University of Texas.

As illustrator and art director, Kasnot has been on both sides of the creative process, an experience he says helps him "know what art directors expect and what illustrators can offer."

David Kimble

In the vanguard of illustration for the automobile world, Kimble works round-the-clock. *Car and Driver* magazine called him "King of the Cutaways, at least automotively" in their April 1995 issue. The same biography describes his start in the field: "Kimble's first serious cutaway was the Halibrand-Shrike car that Eddie Sachs was killed in during the 1964 Indy 500....He has appeared in every major car magazine in the world and has produced nearly 100 cutaways."

As a teenager, Kimble attended Chouinard's Art Institute in Los Angeles. He learned technical drawing at the Academy of Technical Arts and studied engineering at the Pasadena College of the Nazarene. He tried a lot of things before he found his gift for cutaways and a good agent.

Christopher A. Klein

As NATIONAL GEOGRAPHIC's only staff artist at this time, Klein feels a responsibility and a dedication to the mission of the organization—he listens closely to experts and maintains a strong attention to detail and accuracy for all of his work.

Klein's work for NATIONAL GEOGRAPHIC, available through the Society's Image Sales Collection, is often requested for use in other publications. He has won recognition and several awards from such organizations as the Society of Illustrators.

Klein studied illustration at the Cooper Union in New York. Commissioned by art director Bob Teringo to illustrate the Society's historical atlas, *People and Places of the Past*, Klein credits Teringo and researcher Merrill Clift for seeing his potential even though his paintings were not exactly of typical NATIONAL GEOGRAPHIC subjects. His personal art is "photorealism surrealism" in which he creates his own worlds in a very realistic style.

Richard and Kent Leech

Richard Leech studied commercial art in England and began his career in an apprenticeship with Rolls Royce as a technical illustrator. In 1963 he moved to the United States to work freelance for various clients, including Yamaha and Honda. NATIONAL GEOGRAPHIC art directors and researchers enjoyed Richard's profound interest in how things work which led to several pieces for the NATIONAL GEOGRAPHIC. His

death, while illustrating the English Channel Tunnel for the magazine, was mourned by all.

Kent Leech, whose superb drawing skills were partnered with his father's work on the Macon cutaway (title pages) and other illustrations, studied art in London. He continues to develop technical illustrations and to operate the California studio he shared with his father.

Jay Matternes

Art Director Chris Sloan, life-long fan of the art of Jay Matternes, says: "Every Matternes painting is a study. To understand his art you must see that each finished piece represents the artist's intense exploration of his subjects. He goes beyond most artists by actually building his animals from skeleton to muscle, skin, feathers, and fur. Finally adding such elements as environment, attitude, and locomotion, he brings his creatures to life. His obsession with detail and grasp of subtleties endears him to scientists and has made him the foremost painter of ancient mammals of our time."

Matternes's murals hang in the Smithsonian's Museum of Natural History in Washington, D.C. and in the American Museum of Natural History in New York.

Robert T. McCall

As a visual historian for NASA, McCall has illustrated the space program from the early Mercury flights to the space shuttle. For the U.S. Postal Service, he illustrated a 1971 twin stamp, "Decade of Achievement," which was canceled on the moon as worldwide audiences watched on television.

McCall served as conceptual artist for Stanley Kubrick's film, *2001: A Space Odyssey*, the *Star Trek* movies and Disney's *Black Hole*.

He painted a six-story-high mural celebrating the first manned lunar adventure for the National Air and Space Museum in Washington, D.C.

Davis Meltzer

Meltzer's inspiration for art was easy to trace, since his parents were successful still life and landscape painters. Having recently purchased one of his mother's paintings, which draw high prices from collectors, Davis confided, "She'd kill me if she knew how much I paid for it."

Meltzer studied art at Philadelphia's Museum School of Art and worked as a staff artist for the Mel Richman Studios from 1956-1958.

Since then, he has been a freelance

illustrator for advertising agencies, pharmaceutical companies, and publication houses. A large part of his career has been dedicated to the National Geographic Society—books and the magazine—and to NASA for whose educational programs he has illustrated several large wall sheets. Meltzer's work has appeared in *Ranger Rick*, *Reader's Digest*, *Newsweek*, and in books published by Time-Life, Chilton Publishing Company, Macray Smith Publishers and J.B. Lippincott. The U.S. Postal Service commissioned him to illustrate stamps on ballooning and prehistoric animals. Meltzer lives in Huntingdon Valley, Pennsylvania.

Pierre Mion

Assigned to illustrate innovative research work with Jacques Cousteau, Sylvia Earle, and other scientists, Mion's illustrations for the Society cover a variety of topics.

Mion's art education included a 12-year project working with Norman Rockwell on a series of space paintings for *Look* magazine.

Five times he crossed the continent by motorcycle, one of them to conduct solar architecture research for the Smithsonian. Mion is a horseback rider, SCUBA diver, skier, and licensed glider pilot. His fine art, done in oil, acrylic, gouache, watercolor, pastel, or pencil, has been exhibited in more than 15 cities worldwide.

Kirk Moldoff

At the time art director David Seager commissioned him to illustrate the chapter openers for the Society's book *The Incredible Machine*, Moldoff was sculpting medical structures in layers of etched acrylic. Too expensive and time-consuming for the book project, the acrylic model idea was reworked in favor of layers of acetate on an airbrushed background.

Moldoff uses 3-D computer modeling as well as the airbrush technique to visualize how drugs interact with the body at the molecular level.

He created seven panoramic paintings for advertisements for Lederle Laboratories, working with medical researchers to depict their working landscape.

Moldoff received a B.A. in neuroscience from the University of Rochester in 1976 and an M.S. in medical education.

Bruce Morser

The primary reason Morser takes on a variety of illustration assignments is to feed his curiosity about a variety of subjects. He aims to provide his viewers with an opportunity to "get down on their hands and knees and have a read"– just the thing he likes to do himself.

Morser received a B.A. from Colgate University and an M.A. in painting from the University of Washington. He has a minor in geology, an interest rekindled by his work on the diagram of barrier island movement (pages 78-79).

Morser's clients include Boeing, NASA, Microsoft, and Starbucks. In his fine art subjects and his illustrations for high-tech clients, Morser enjoys the research and firsthand experience with innovative machines not available to the general public.

He is an avid rower and skier and enjoys cruising his 50-year-old wooden sailboat.

Carl Rohrig

"Rohrig lives in West Germany. He has illustrated several books and articles, including pieces for *Stern* magazine and *Geo*." (biographical paragraph from *The Incredible Machine*, 1986).

Richard Schlecht

Schlecht developed an expertise in underwater archaeology and maritime history by reconstructing many sunken ships. It took studying 20 hours of film footage, frame by frame, and Schlecht's knowledge of 19th-century wooden warships to reconstruct a pair of wrecks from the War of 1812 found on the bottom of Lake Ontario.

On dry land, he employed the same technique, working with Colonial Williamsburg archaeologist Ivor Nöel Hume to recreate Wolstenholme Towne.

Schlecht has also worked for Time-Life Books, illustrating seven volumes of *The Seafarers* series. Each volume contained an eight-page portfolio of Schlecht's drawings depicting milestones in maritime history. He credits his work with American naval architect and historian William Avery Baker for his inspiration in historical reconstruction as well as his dedication to good research practices.

Schlecht has illustrated more than two dozen stamps for the U.S. Postal Service and numerous historical reconstructions for the National Park Service.

Awards from the Society of Illustrators, *Communications Arts* magazine, and other organizations have recognized Schlecht's work over

his three decades as an illustrator.

Ned Seidler

As a staff artist at the National Geographic Society from 1967 until he retired in 1985, Seidler captured in his paintings the essence of discovery and exploration. His talent for realistic renderings captivates readers on topics ranging from life in a mountain stream to the routes of the *Bounty* and *Pandora*.

Although officially retired, Seidler continues to paint. Projects include stamps with the U.S. Postal Service and National Geographic Society publications. Seidler and his wife Rosalie won a Silver Medal from the Society of Illustrators for their illustrations for a National Geographic Society pop-up book for children.

Seidler has been honored with a one-artist show at the Society of Illustrators and by inclusion of his work in an exhibition at the Brandywine Museum. He attended the Art Students League and Pratt Institute, where he and his wife Rosalie were classmates.

Rosalie Seidler

Seidler won a Christopher Medal for *Panda Cake*, a book she conceived and illustrated. She is a portrait painter and a self-described "dabbler in various things." She has worked with her husband, Ned, on many articles and books for the National Geographic Society.

The collaboration between them is reinforcing, both artists admit. Rosalie's studio is at the opposite end of their Long Island home from Ned's. With different ways of seeing and expressing what is seen, they "cast off pieces of advice" to each other. Days later, they come to an agreement— when one realizes the other has the best solution for how to handle a visual problem.

Barron Storey

A natural teacher and innovative artist, Storey currently works with students at San Jose State University in documentary illustration. He also has taught illustration at the School of Visual Arts and Pratt Institute in New York, Syracuse University, and the California College of Arts and Crafts, among other schools. He enjoys illustrating complex scientific concepts using innovative approaches.

Corporate clients include Chevron, Conoco, IBM, Sony, McDonald's, Coca-Cola, and Paramount Pictures. His editorial work includes

14 covers commissioned for *Time* magazine and several stories for NATIONAL GEOGRAPHIC.

Storey has been honored with one-artist shows at the Society of Illustrators in New York, winning their highest honor in 1976, and the Fobbo Gallery in San Francisco. He painted a permanent mural installation for the American Museum of Natural History in New York.

Lloyd Kenneth Townsend, Jr.

Townsend was on staff at the Society from 1968 to 1978, illustrating articles on archaeology and science, when he decided to start his freelance business. In addition to Society books and magazines, his clients included the National Park Service, *Smithsonian* magazine, *Reader's Digest*, Time-Life Books and various advertising agencies.

Moving to Maytown, Pennsylvania, with his wife and two children in 1980, Townsend's freelance work extended to more clients. To assist in the work production, he hired assistant artists and sometimes mentored student interns. He now lives in Harrisburg, Pennsylvania.

Joe Tucciarone

Interstellar Illustrations, the name of Tucciarone's creative studio,

describes his focus on astronomical art. A one-man show of his paintings, "Visions of the Universe," is currently touring the United States, Canada, and the United Kingdom. In addition to NATIONAL GEOGRAPHIC magazine and *Frontline of Discovery: Science on the Brink of Tomorrow*, a National Geographic Society book, Tucciarone's work has been published in *Discover, Science, Sky and Telescope*, and Isaac Asimov's *Library of the Universe* series.

Tucciarone earned a M.S. in physics from the University of Toledo. In addition to painting, he teaches astronomy and physical science at Daytona Beach (Florida) Community College.

Rob Wood

Wood graduated from East Tennessee State University and earned a Master's degree from the University of Georgia in graphic design and painting.

He works with technical subject matter for clients that include the National Air and Space Museum, St. Remy Press, and National Geographic books and maps.

Wood has been in the illustration field for 28 years and is currently senior vice president and illustration director for the design and illustration firm of Wood Ronsaville Harlin.

Acknowledgements and Thanks

The Book Division wishes to thank the following people for their valuable assistance in helping this book take shape: NATIONAL GEOGRAPHIC magazine Editor Bill Allen for his continued support of the Art Department; the magazine's illustrations and layout editors who expertly integrate the diagrams into the articles; retired Art Director Howard Paine for his many proposals for such a book over the last 20 years; and art director Jeff Osborn for his helpful input on the final selection of diagrams.

The Book Division extends special thanks to the Legends Division of NATIONAL GEOGRAPHIC magazine, whose original captions were adapted for this book. A staff of talented writers, charged with condensing enormous amounts of information into a few paragraphs, crafted the text blocks for the original publications. Complete accuracy of the original captions was ensured by the Research Division, which carefully checked all the material contained in the text.

Composition for this book by the National Geographic Society Book Division. Printed and bound by R.R. Donnelley & Sons, Willard,. OH. Color separations by Quad/Graphics, Inc., Martinsburg, WV. Dust jacket printed by Miken Systems, Inc., Cheektowaga, NY.

Visit the Society Web site at **www.nationalgeographic.com**